AF326749

In June of 2021 after hearing a great deal about the **Museum of Humanity** and the work of photographer **Ruben Timman** in transforming a site where the military had once produced bombs and grenades into a place that currently honors humanity and the common good in all . . . we knew that on our next trip to the Netherlands a visit to the museum was a must.

Since 2019, thousands of people have experienced this permanent, multi-cultural and breathtaking tribute in Amsterdam as well as engaging with various pop-up exhibits around the world.

In addition more than 5000 students have taken part in the **School of Humanity**, an educational part of the museum.

These are just a handful of the images that I made during my afternoon visit. Enjoy!

I encourage you to **visit, support & learn** from the heart and passion behind this project . . . most of all get out of your personal silo and get to know those living around you.

Most often you will see yourself . . .

Respect, Love & Blessings,

Tim B. Gilman

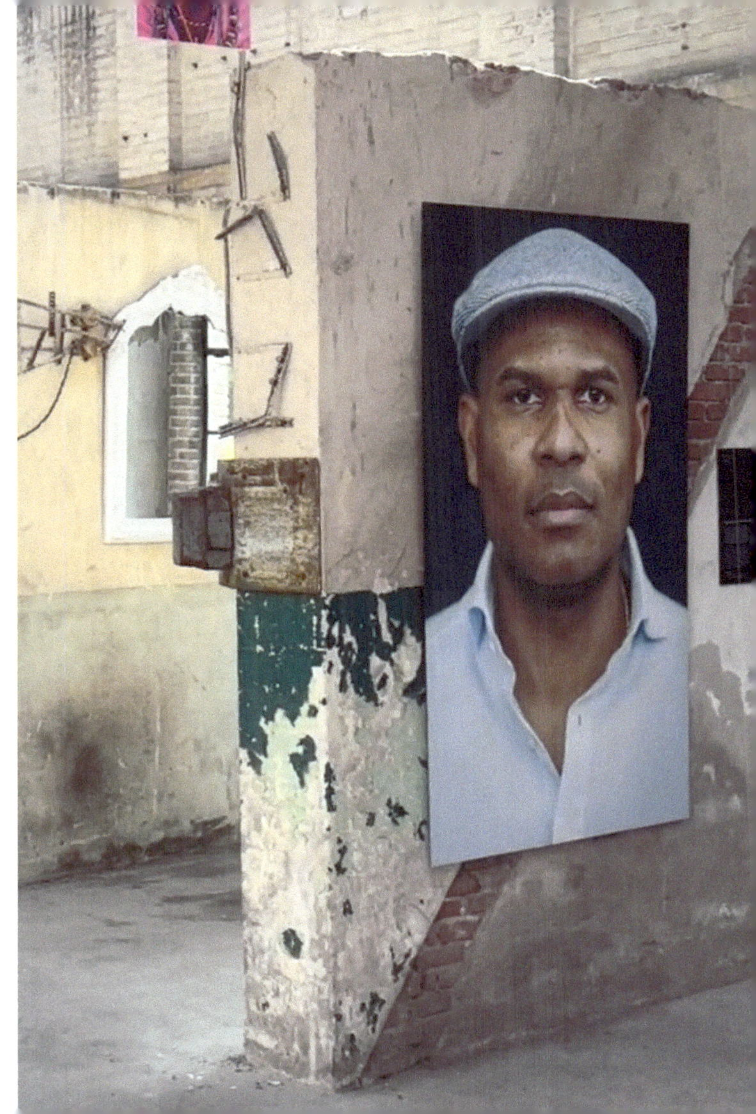

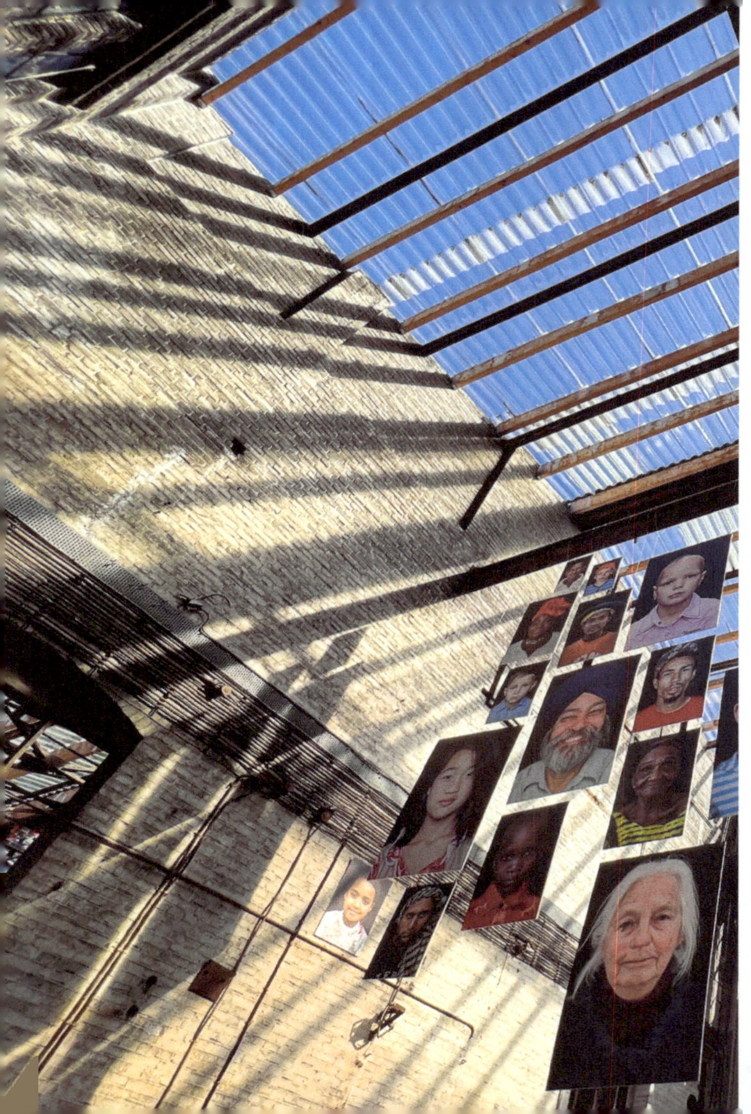

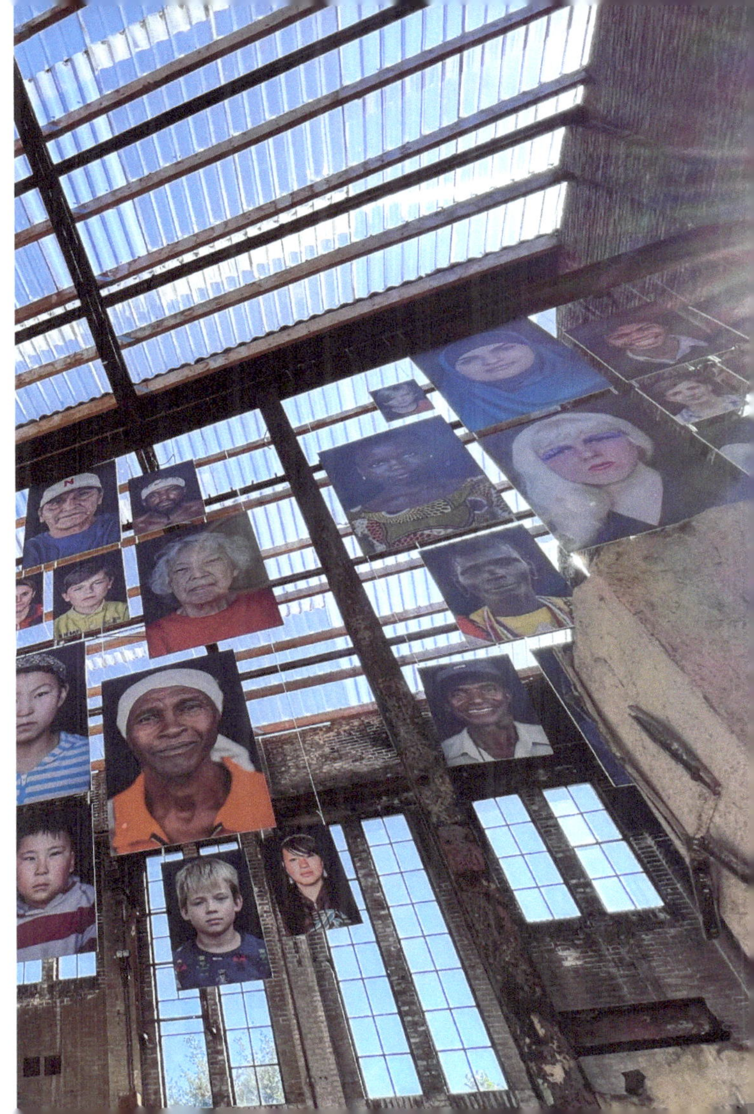

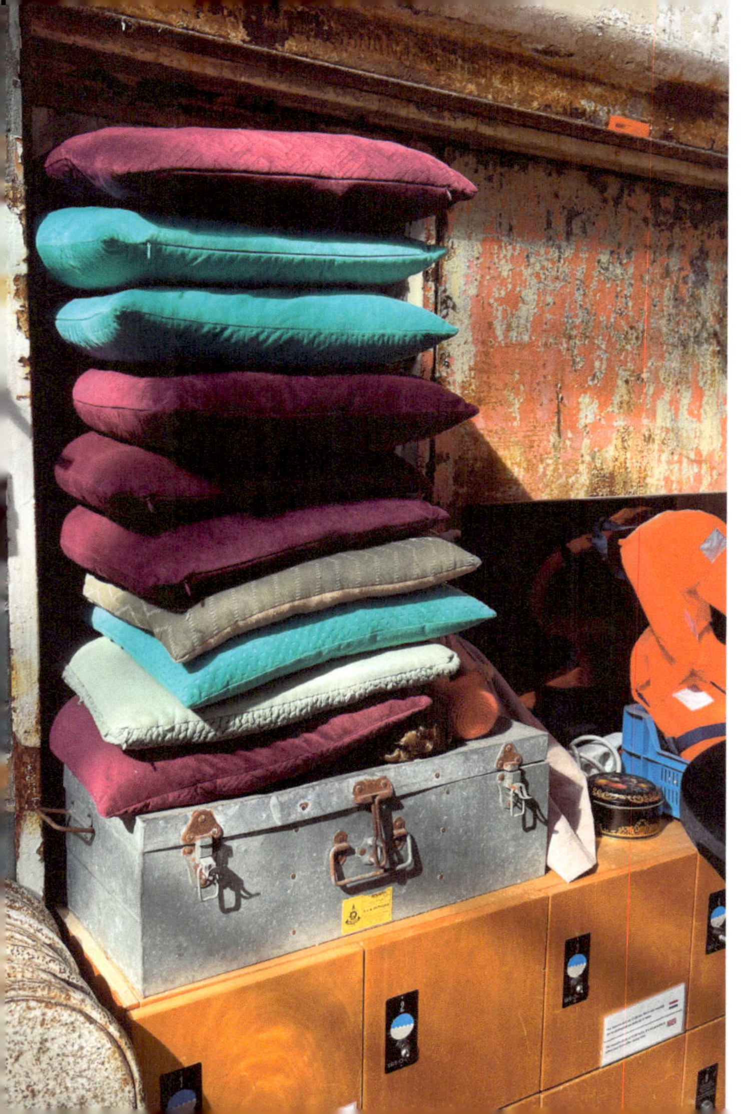

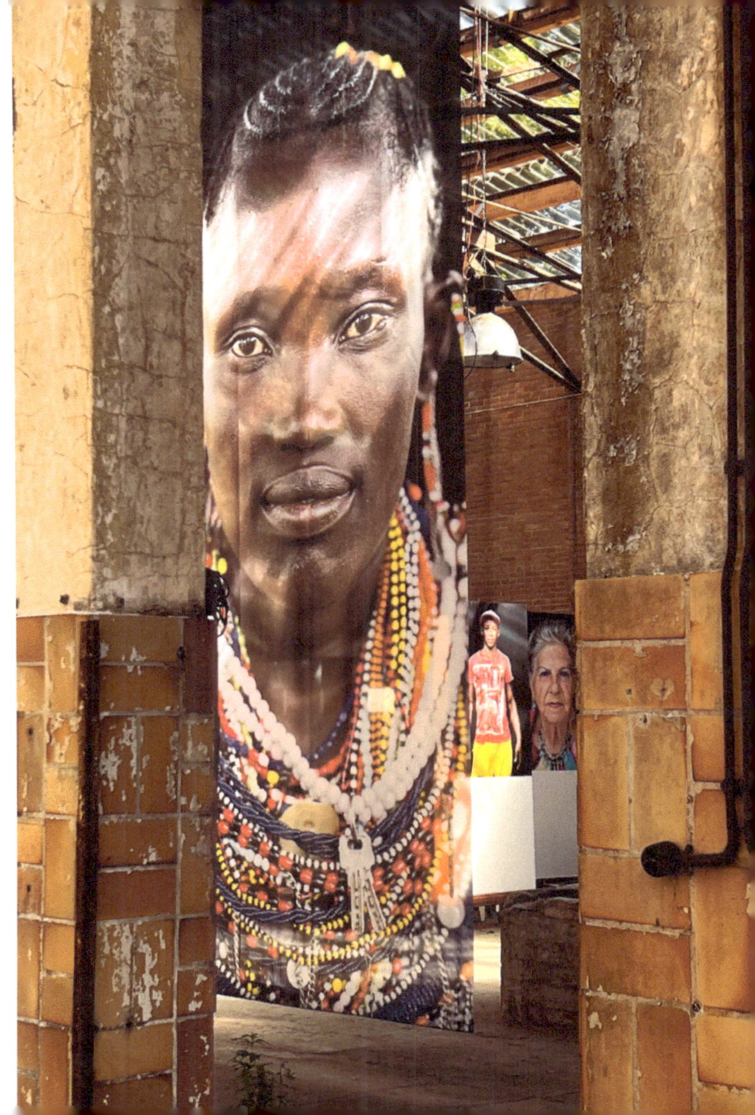

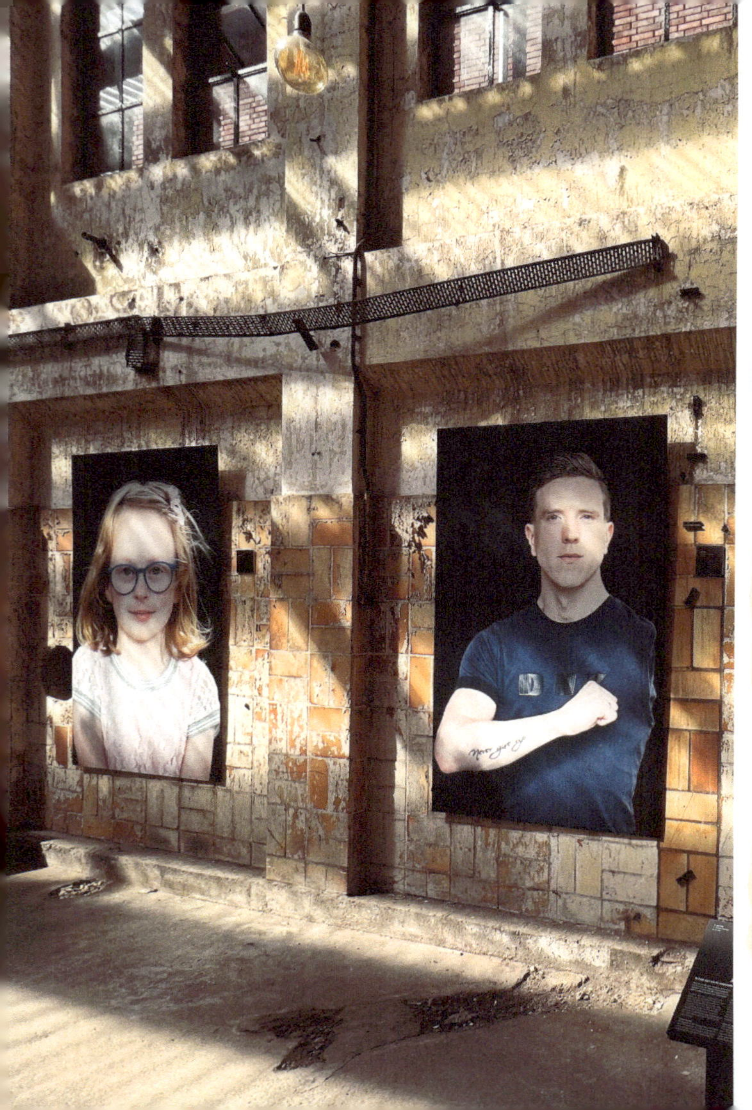

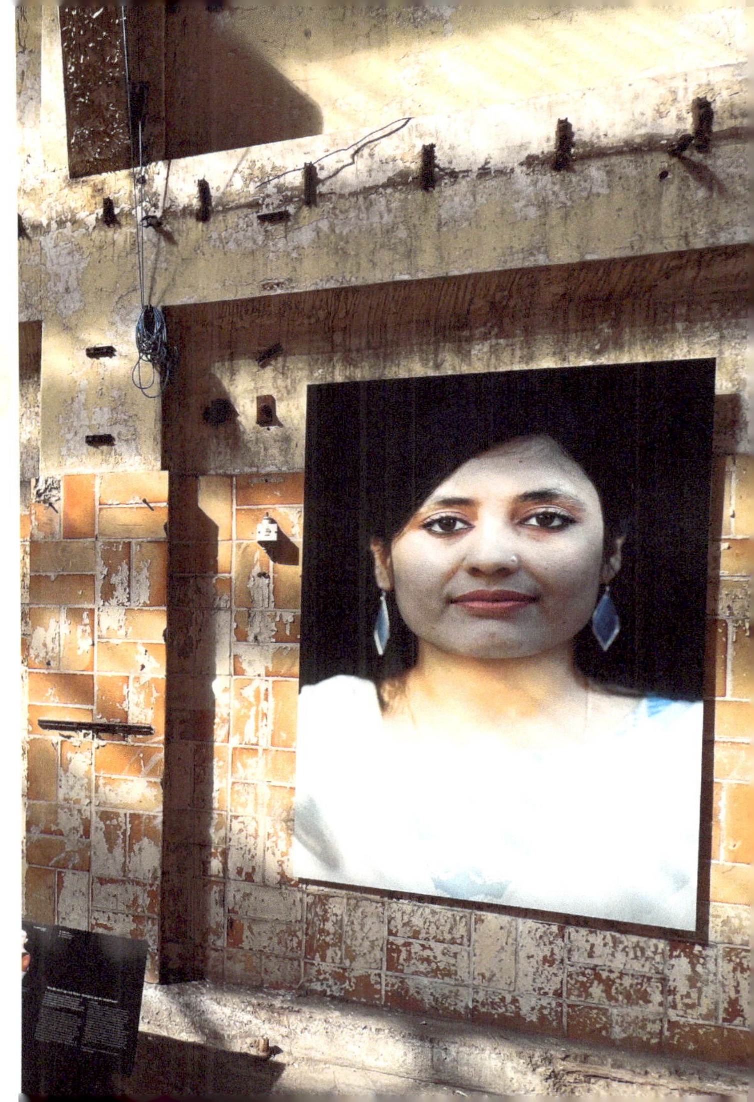

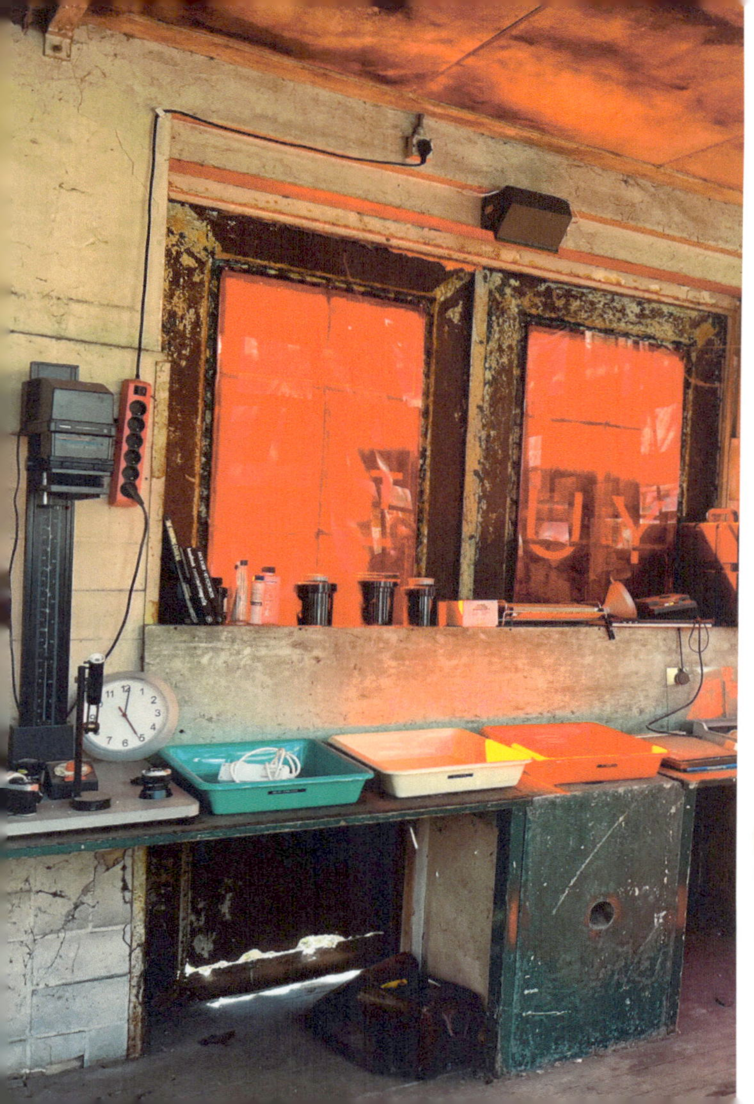

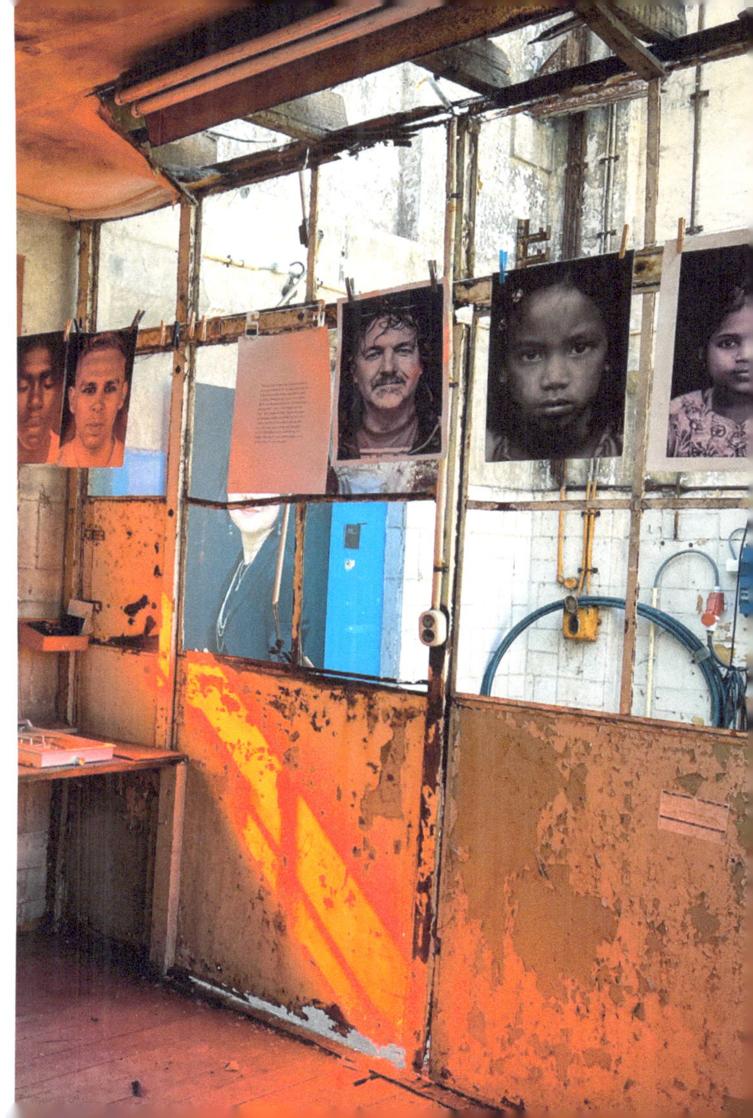

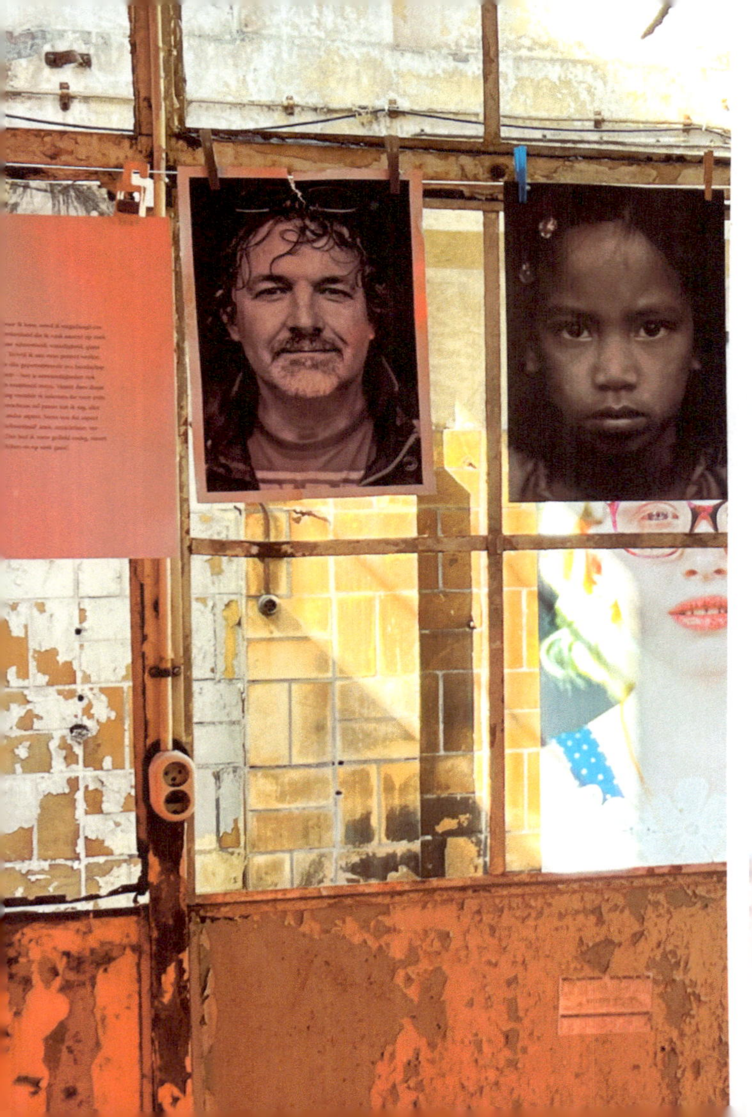

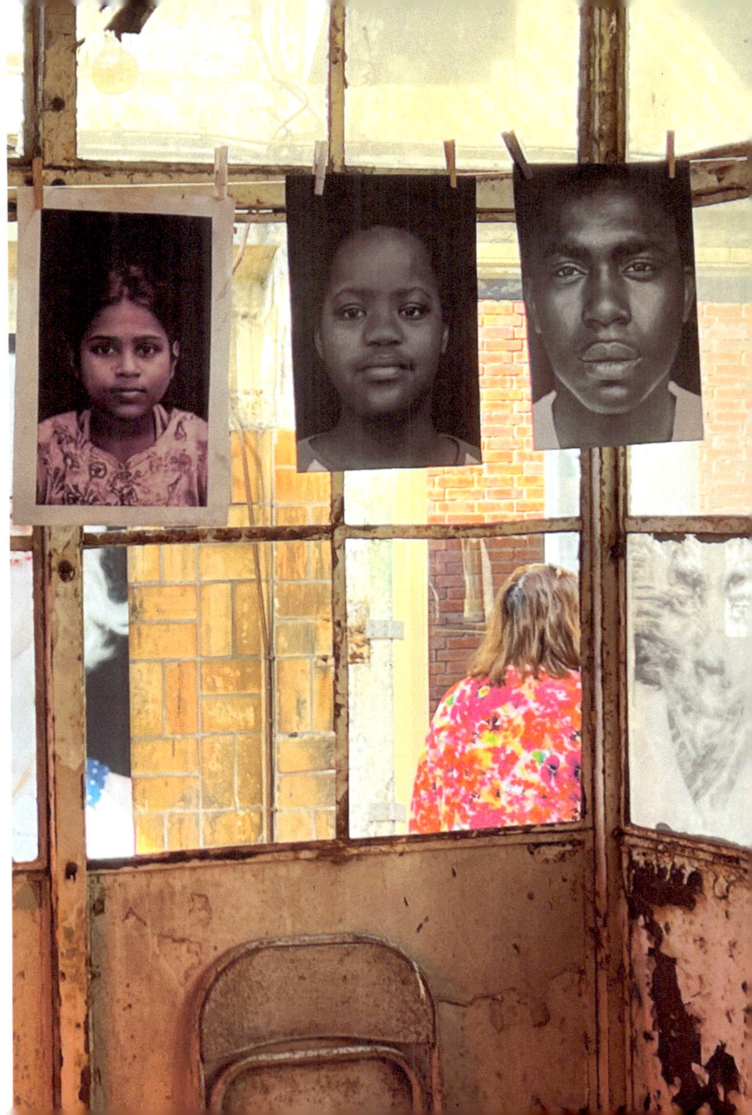

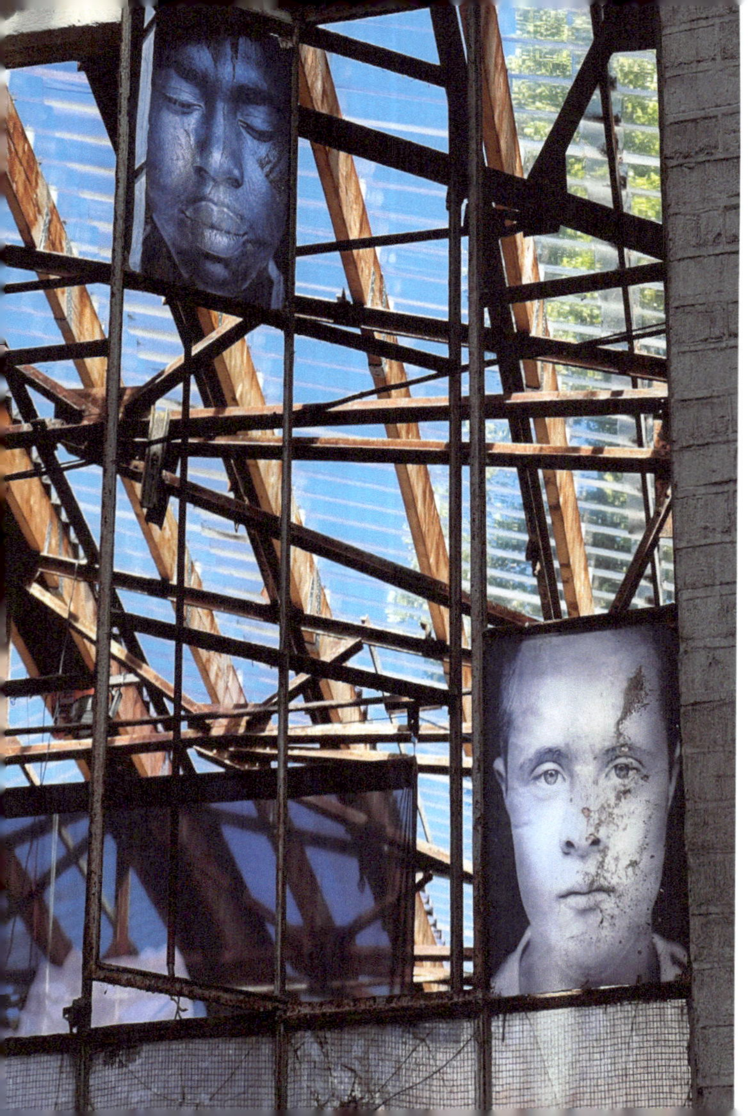

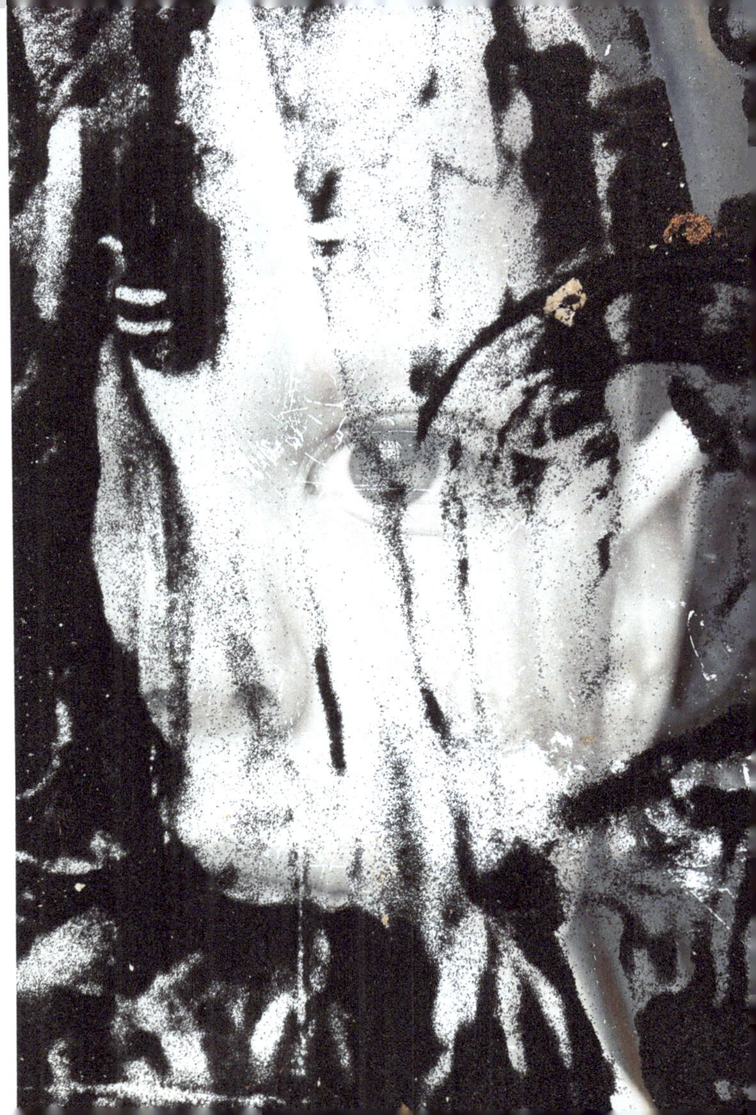

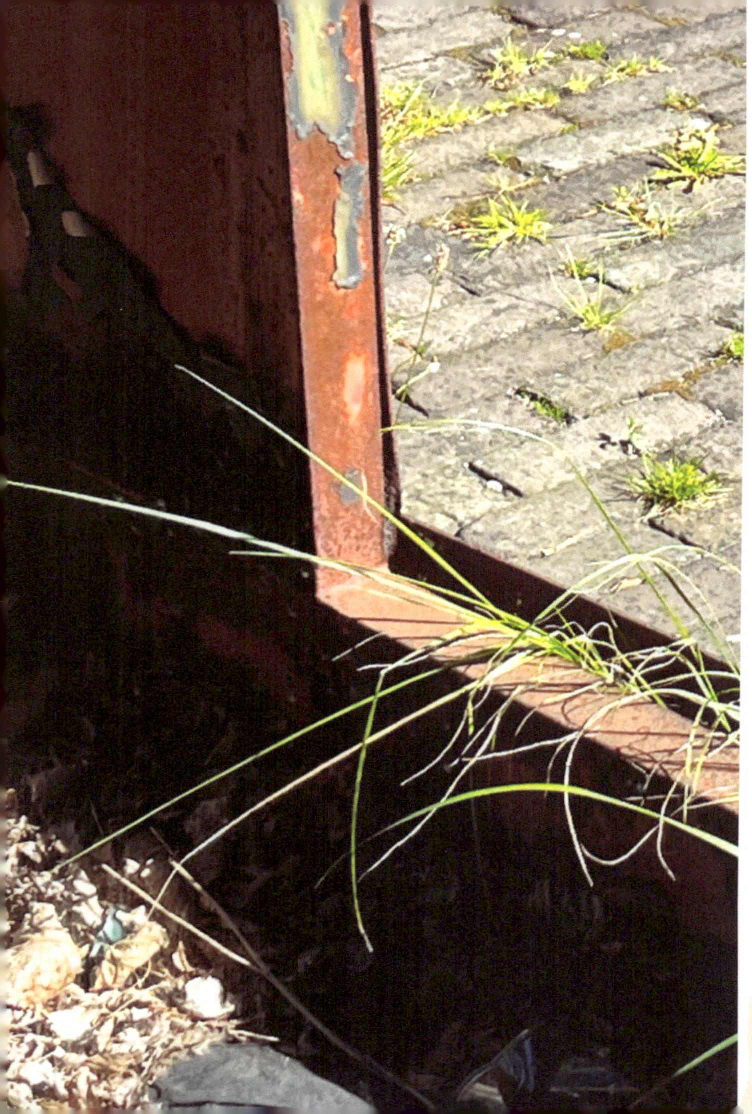

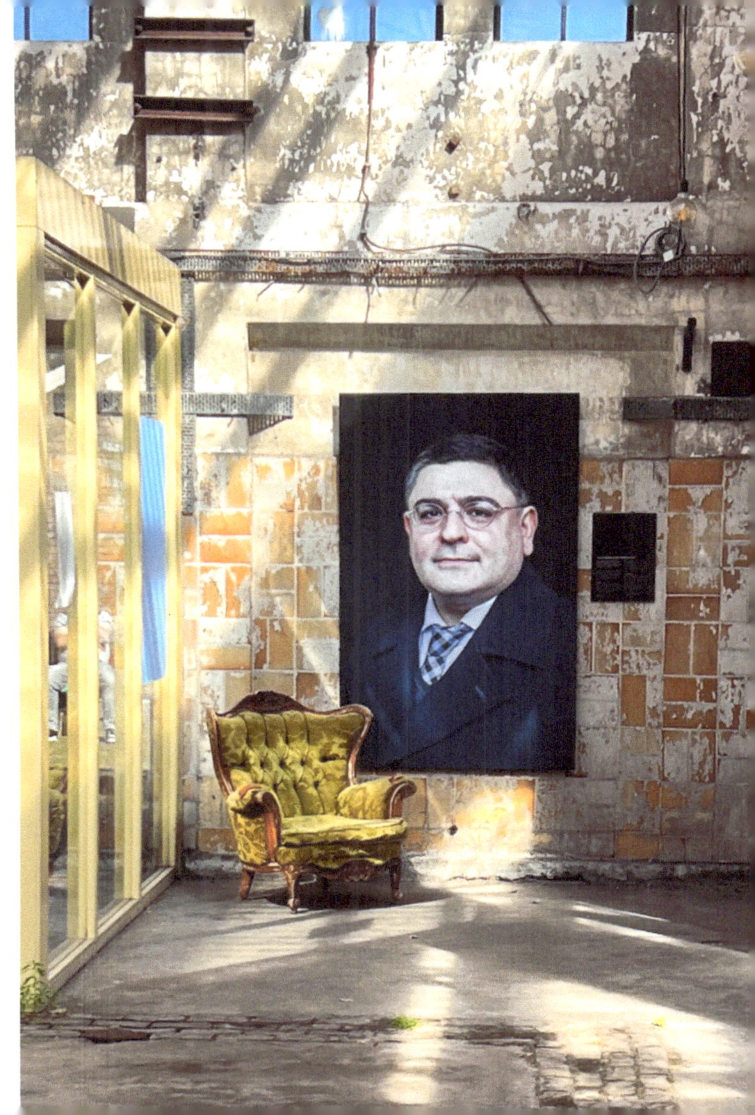

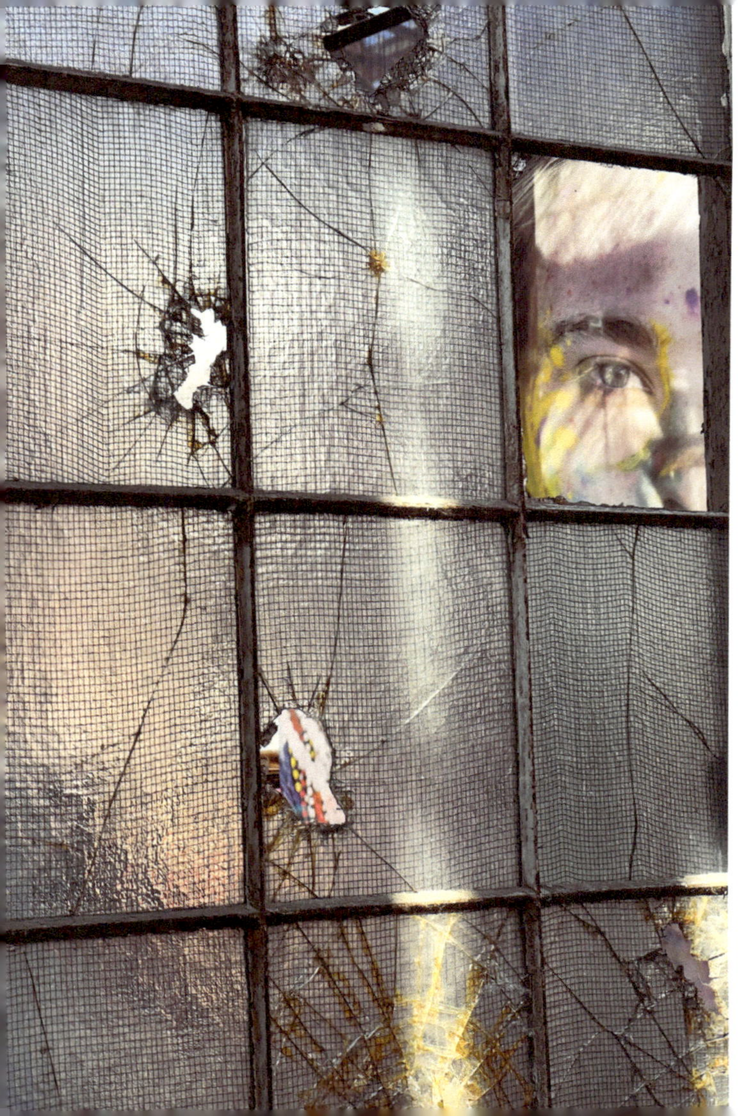

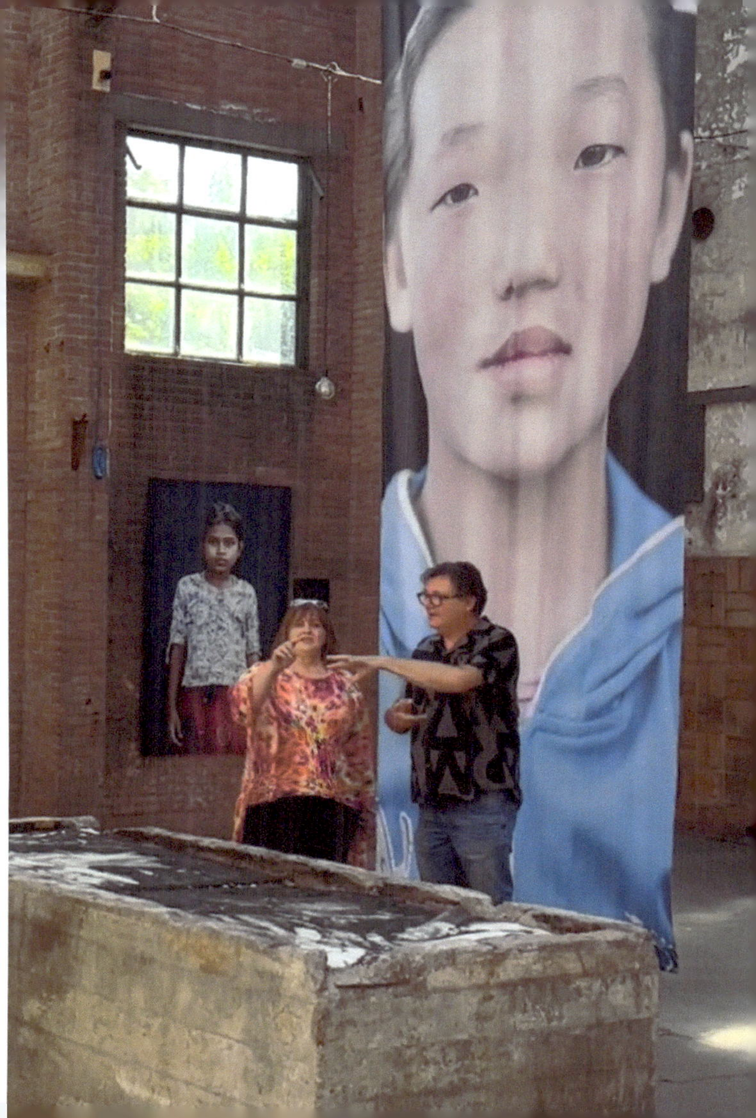

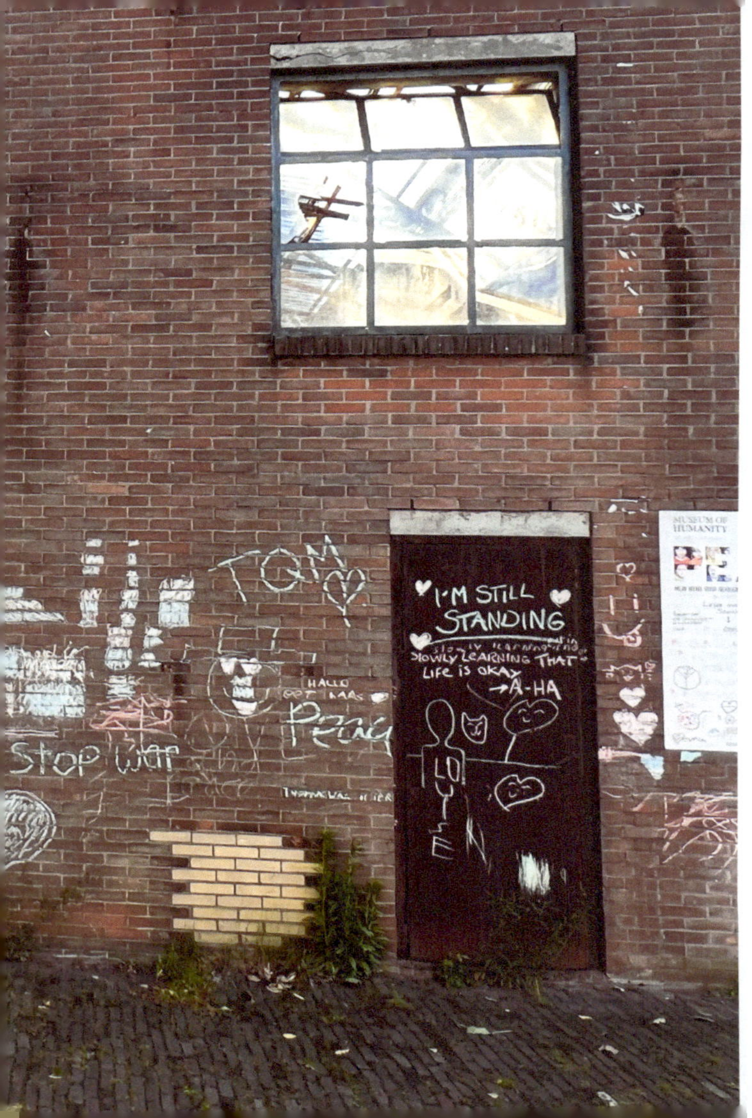
TOM
HALLO
stop war
I'M STILL
STANDING
Slowly Learning that
life is okay
→ A-HA
MUSEUM OF
HUMANITY

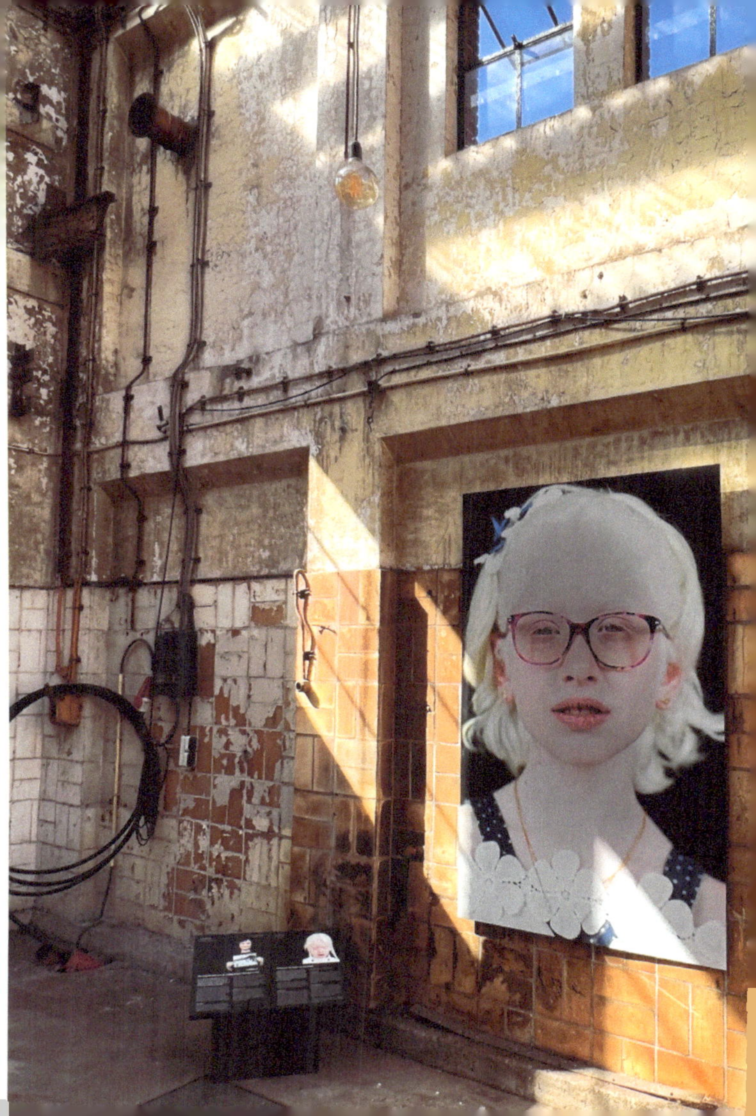

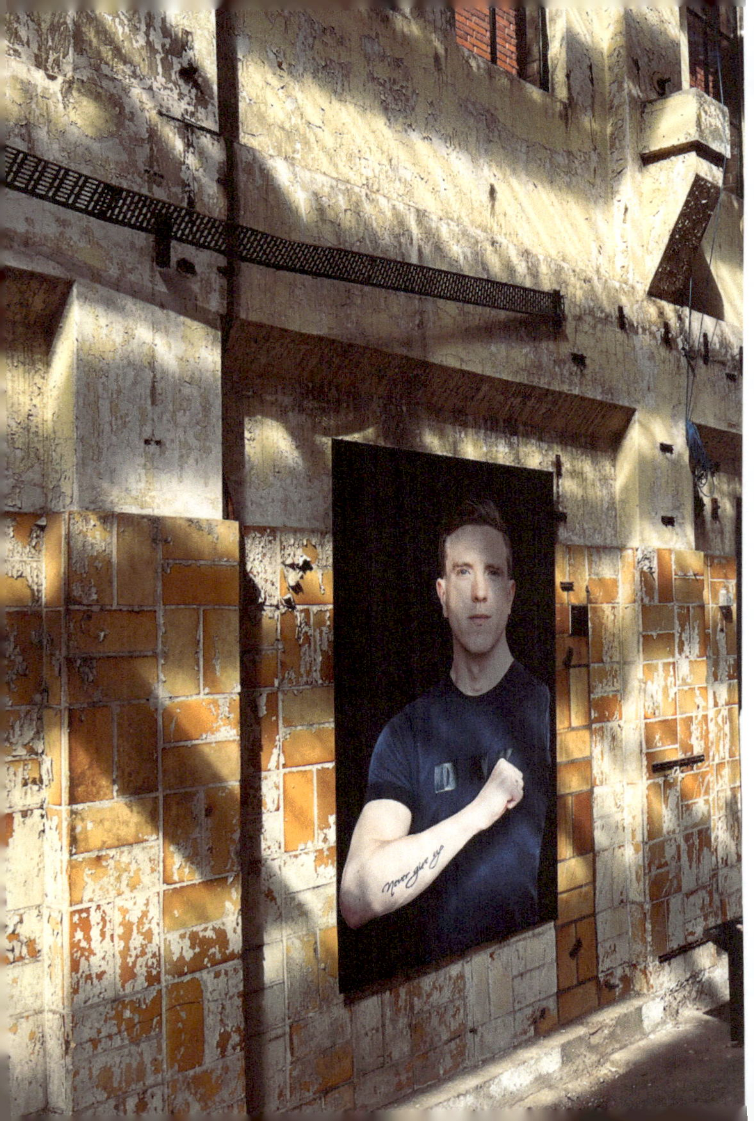
Never give up

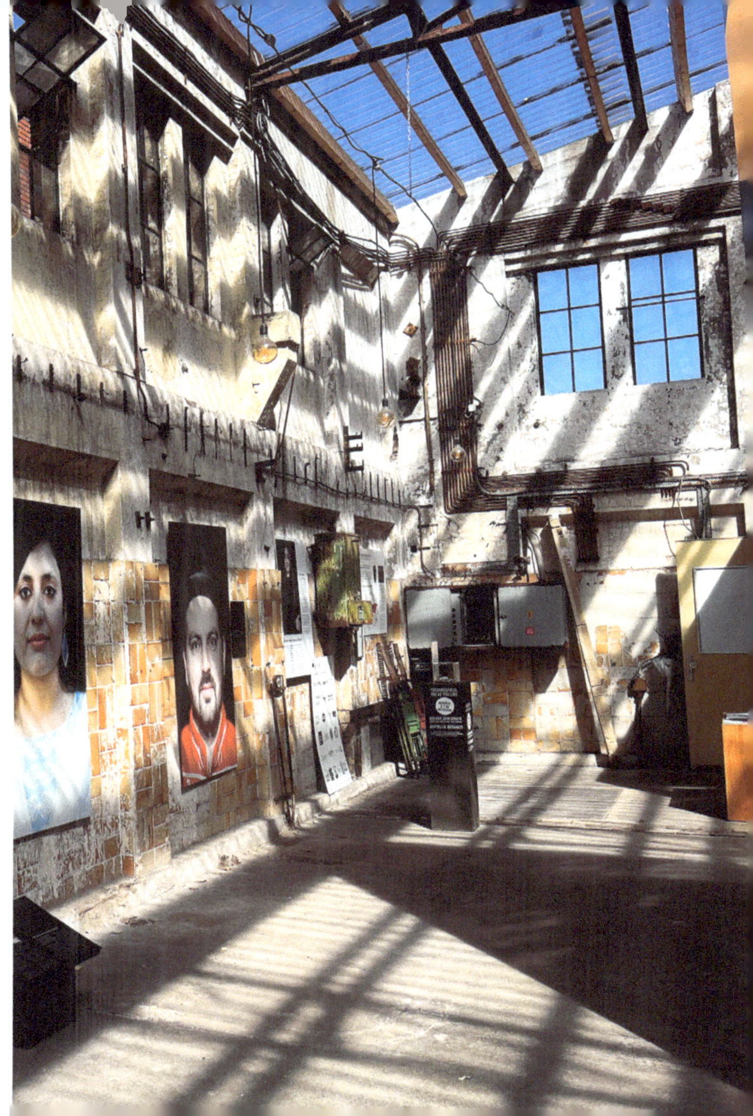

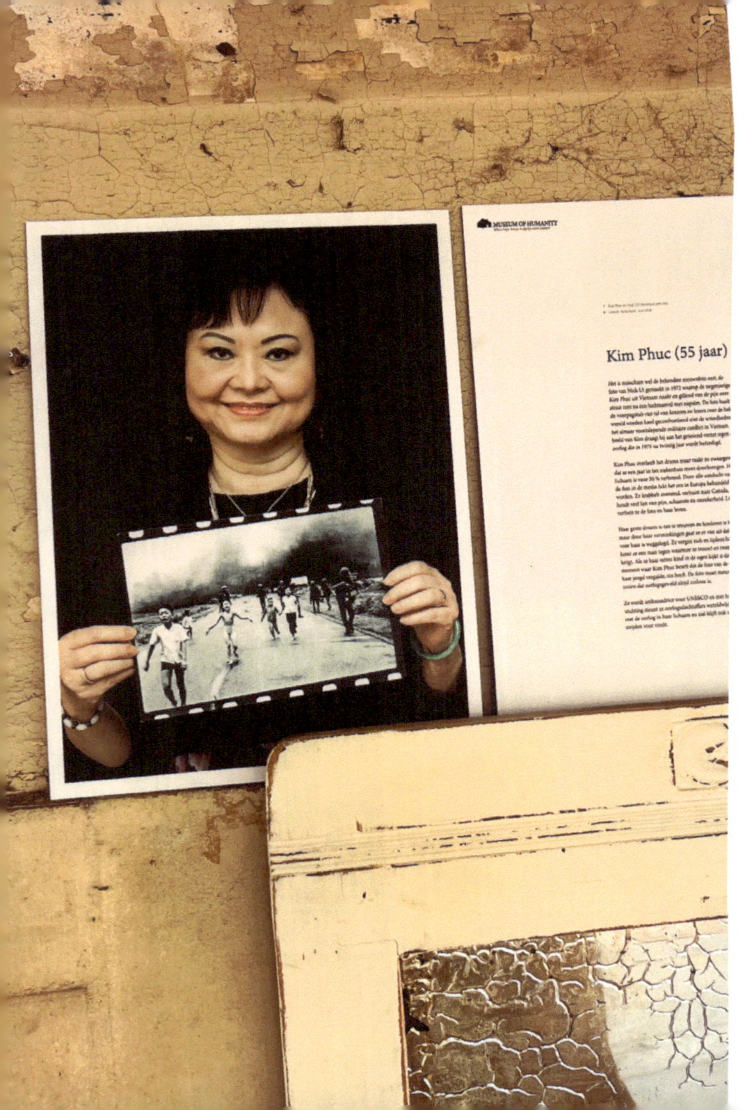

MUSEUM OF HUMANITY
Kim Phuc (55 jaar)

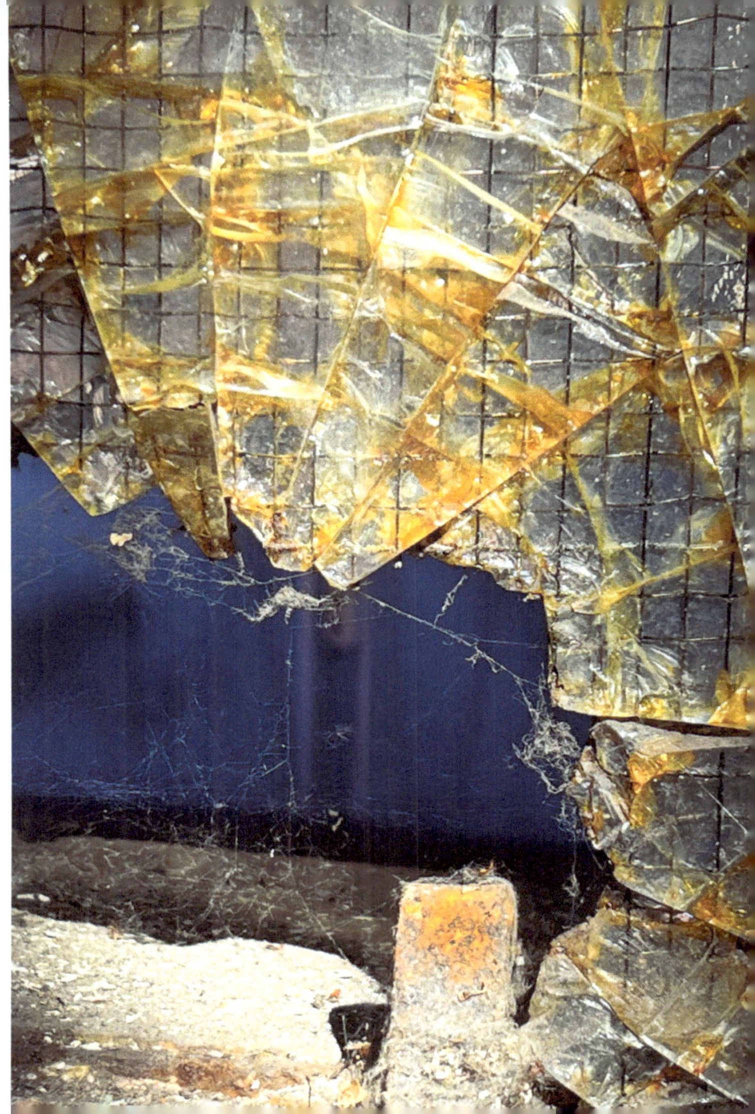

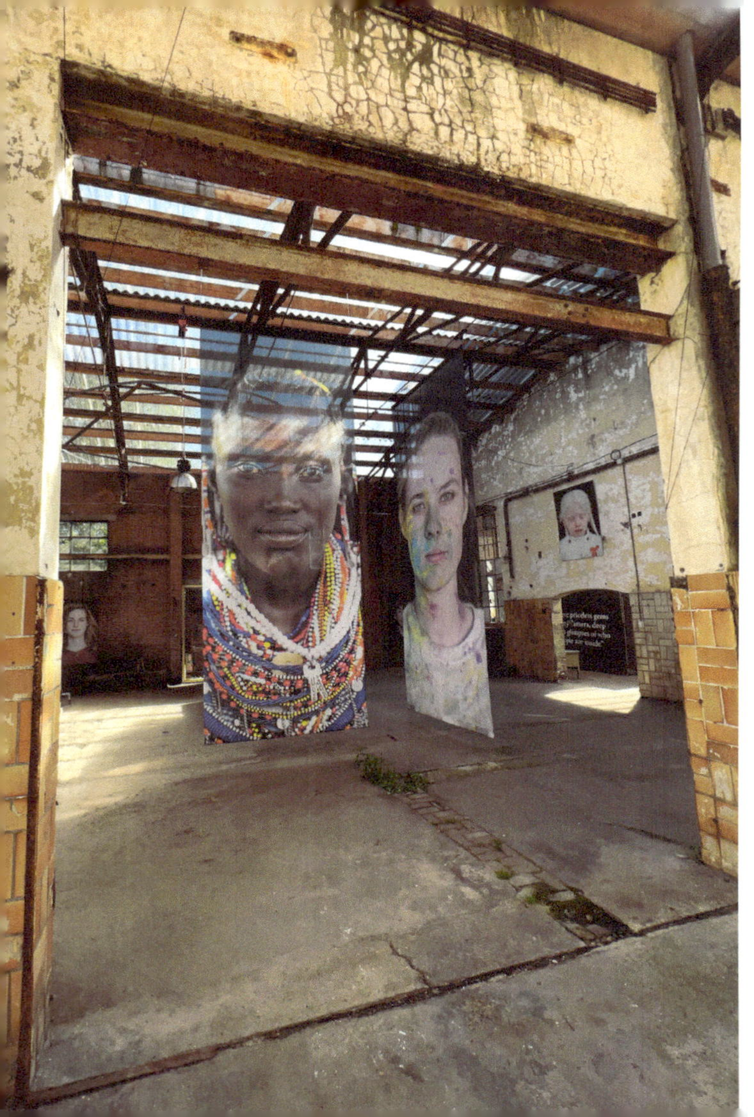

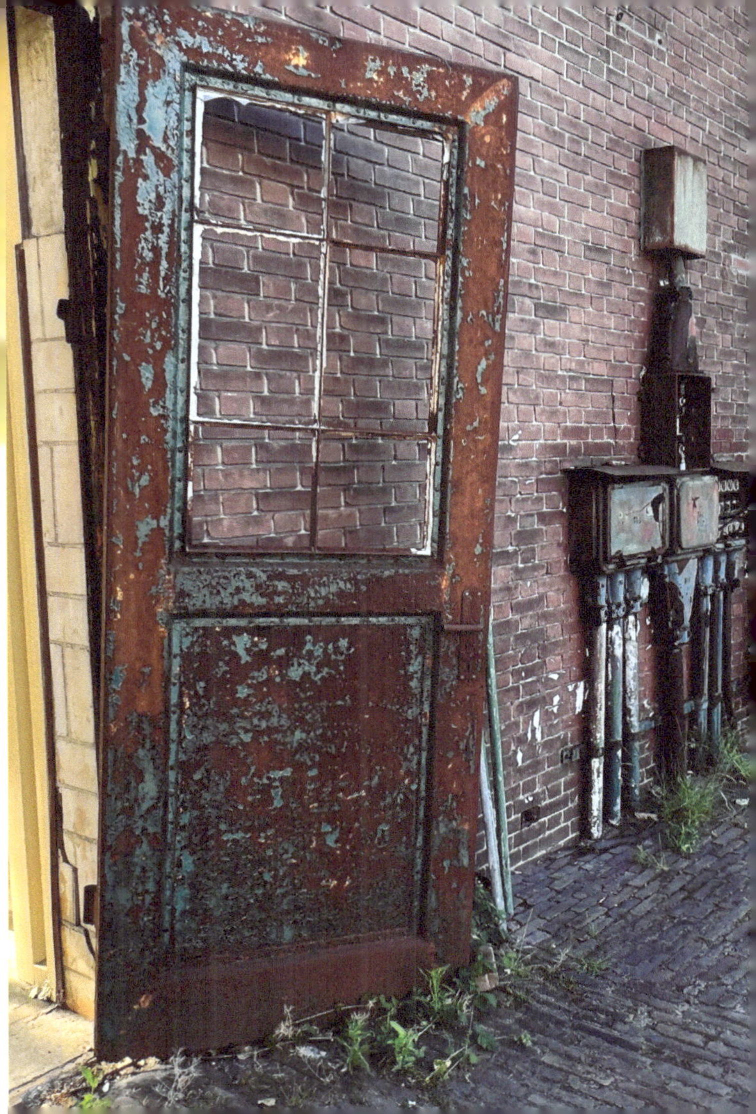

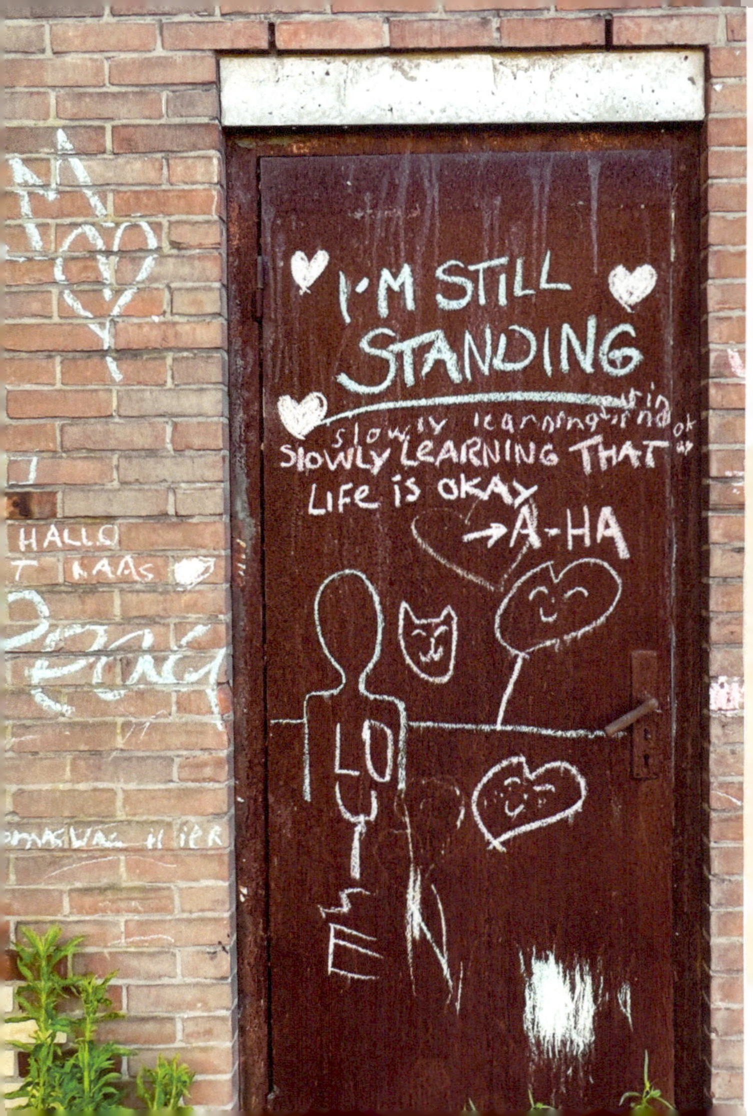

MY
HALLO
T KAAS
OMASWAL HIER
I'M STILL STANDING
slowly learning that
slowly LEARNING THAT ok
LIFE IS OKAY
→ A-HA
LOVE

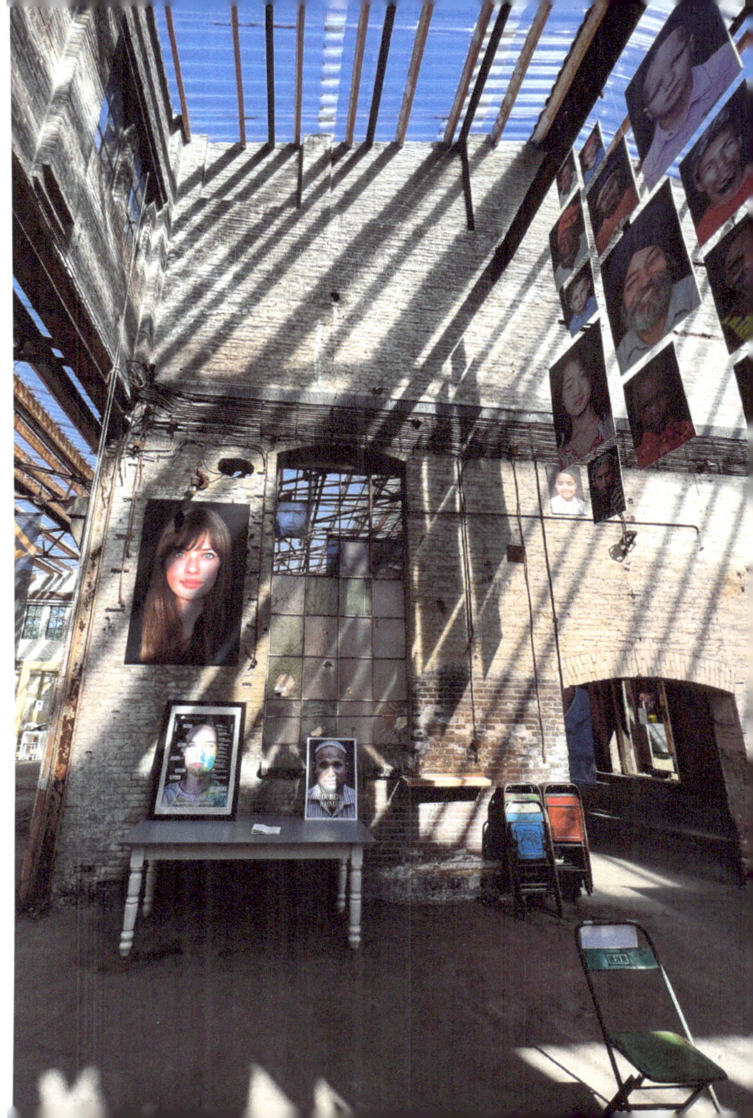

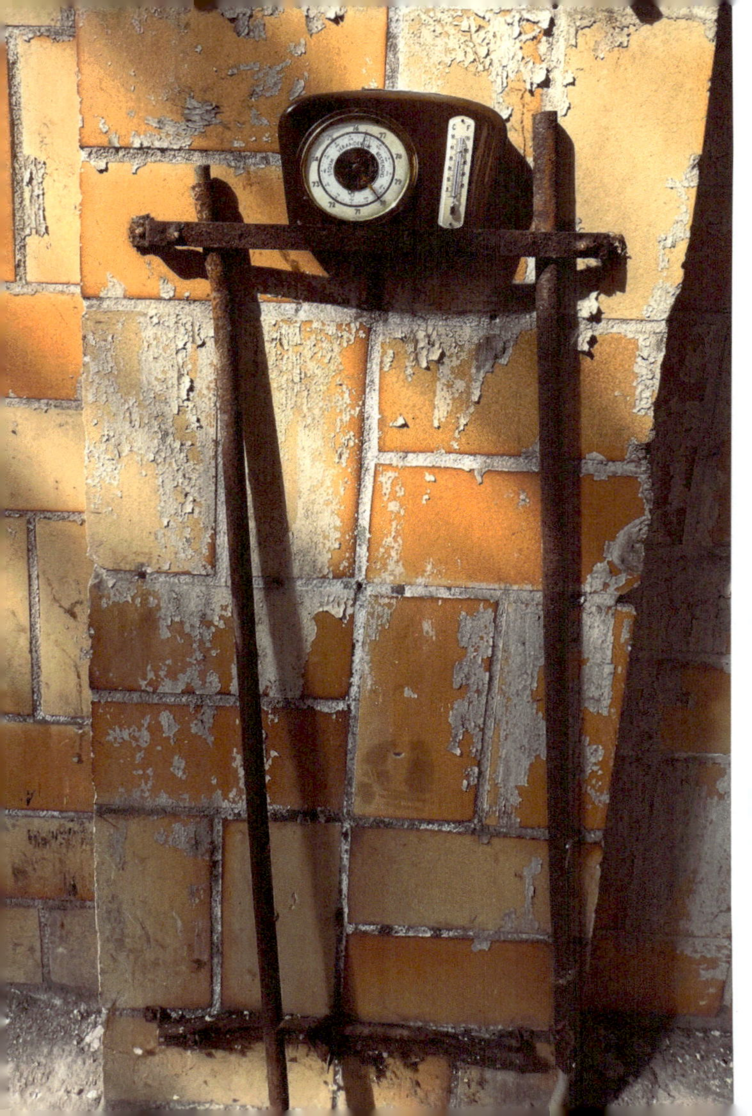

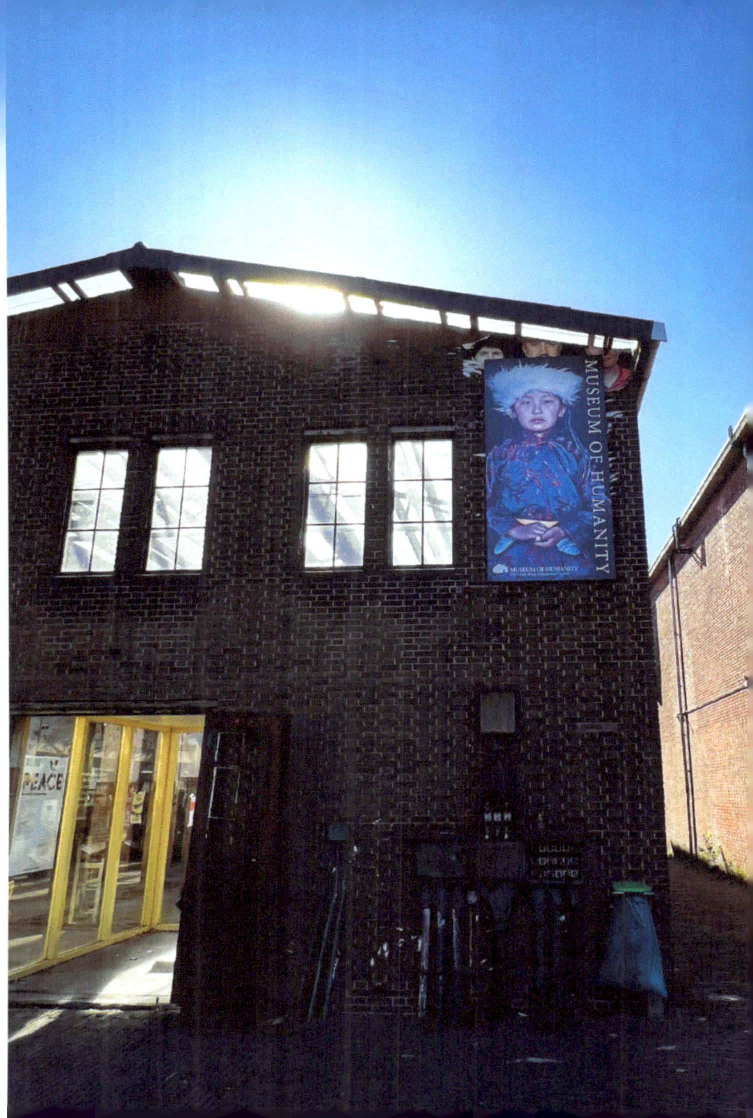
MUSEUM OF HUMANITY
MUSEUM OF HUMANITY
PEACE

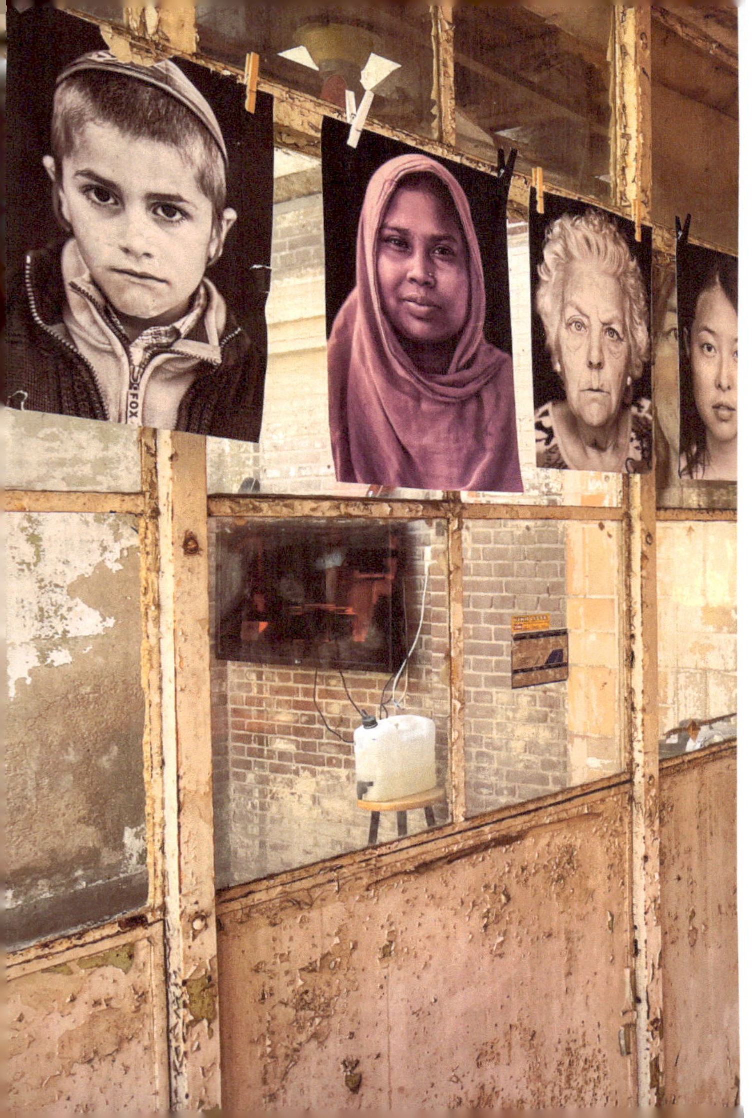

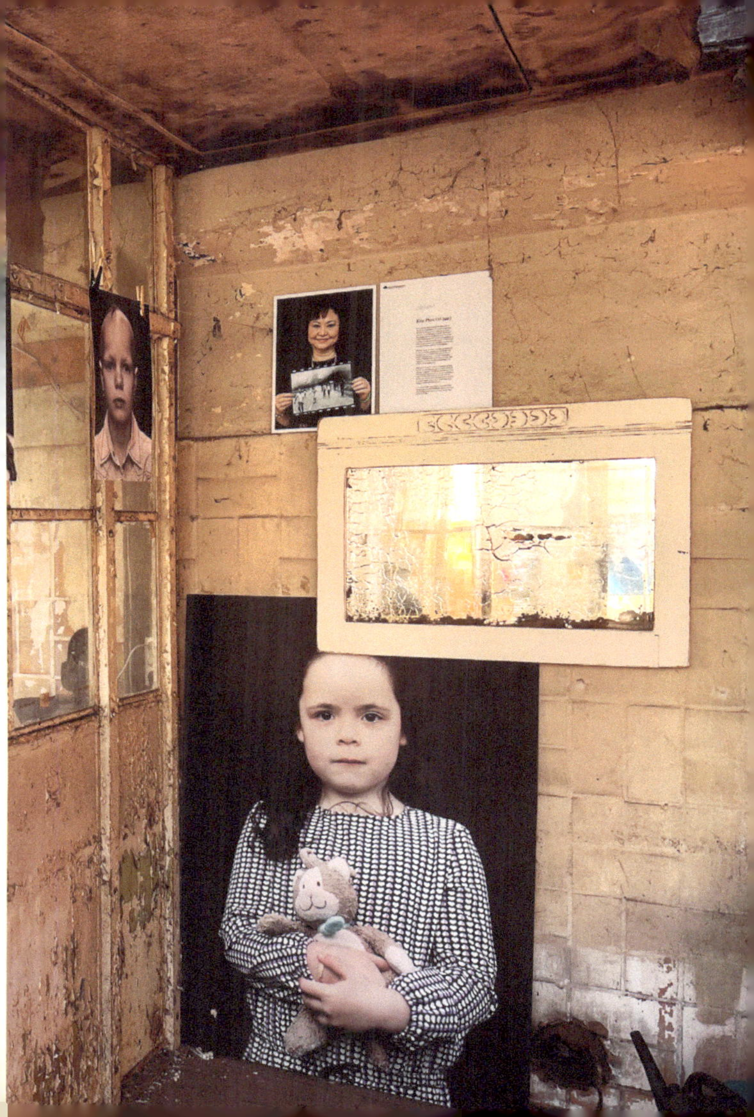

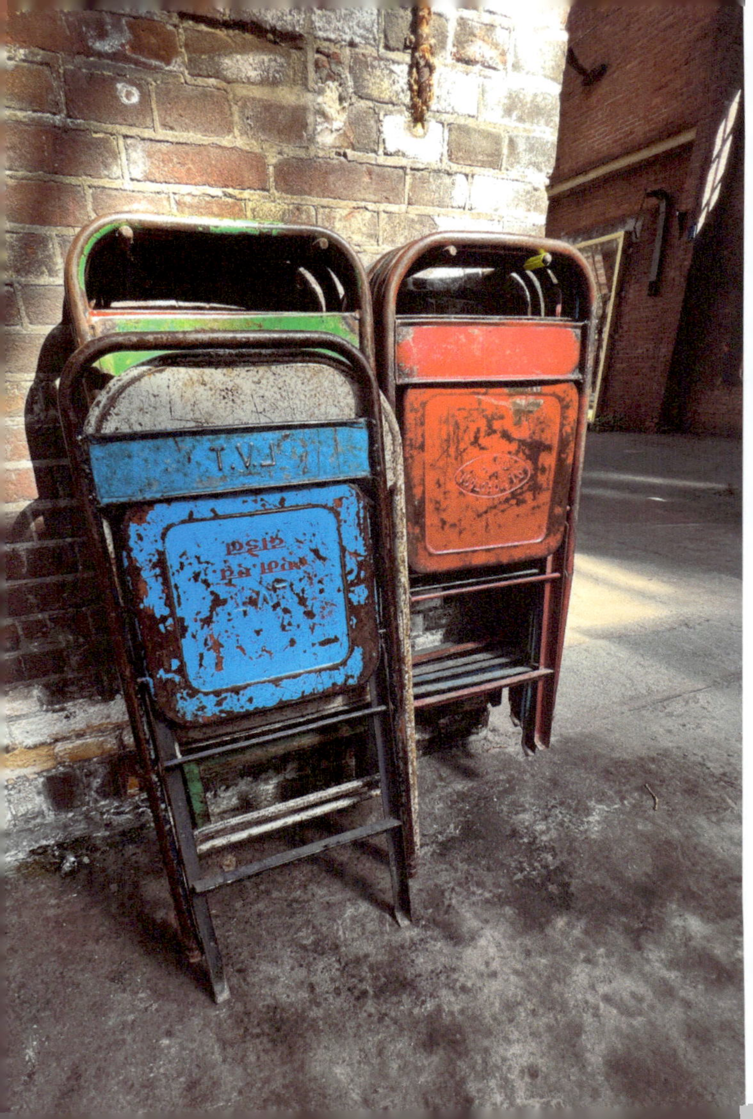

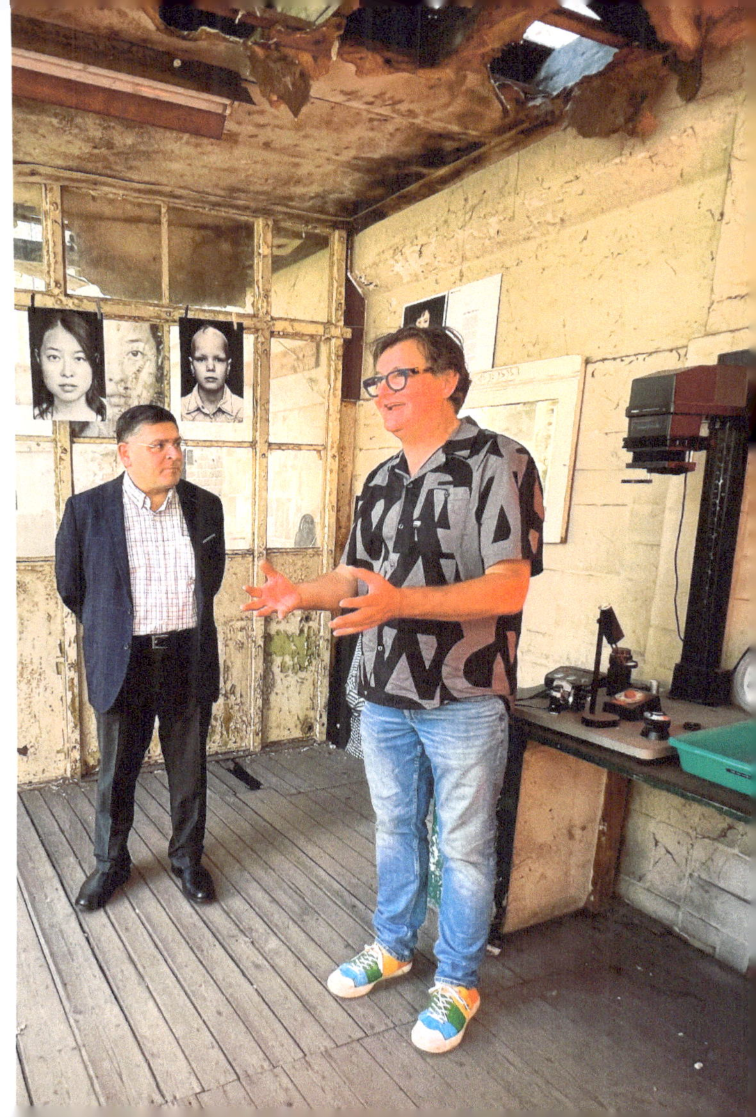

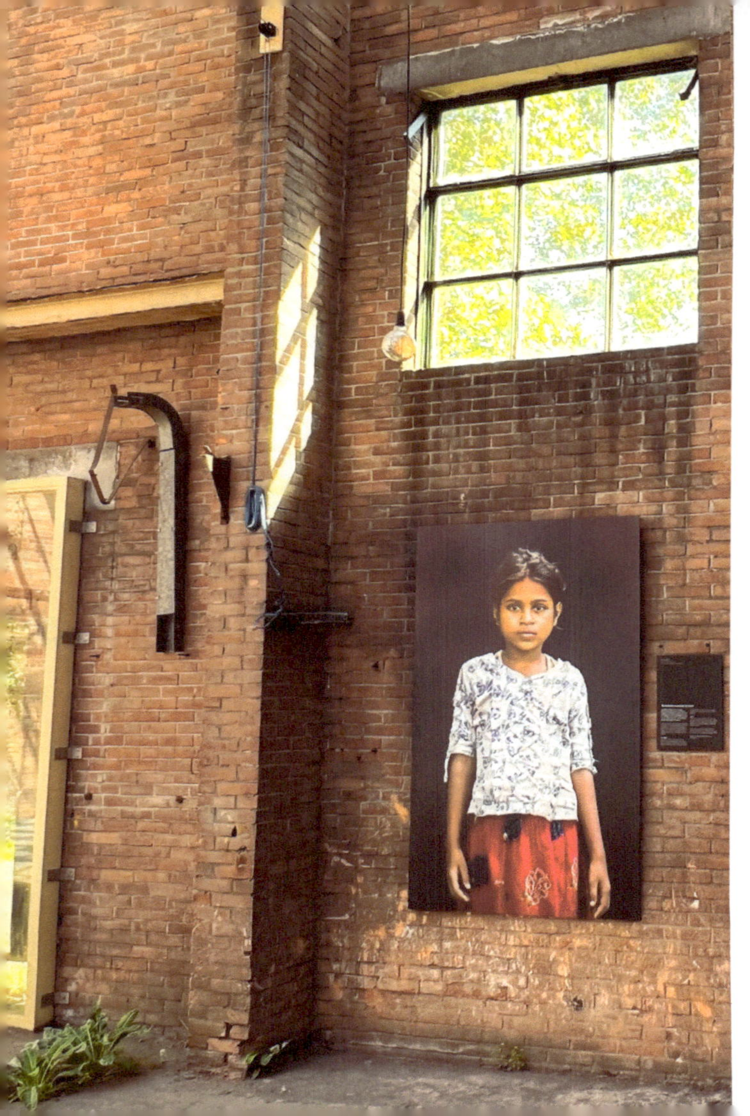

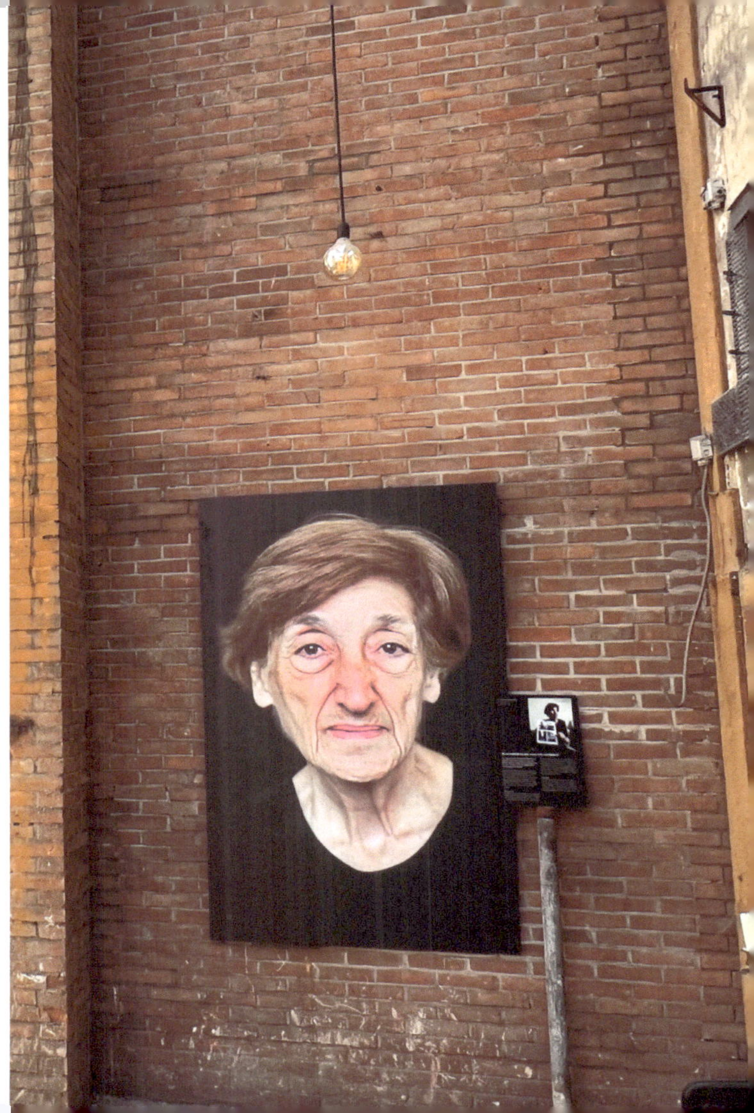

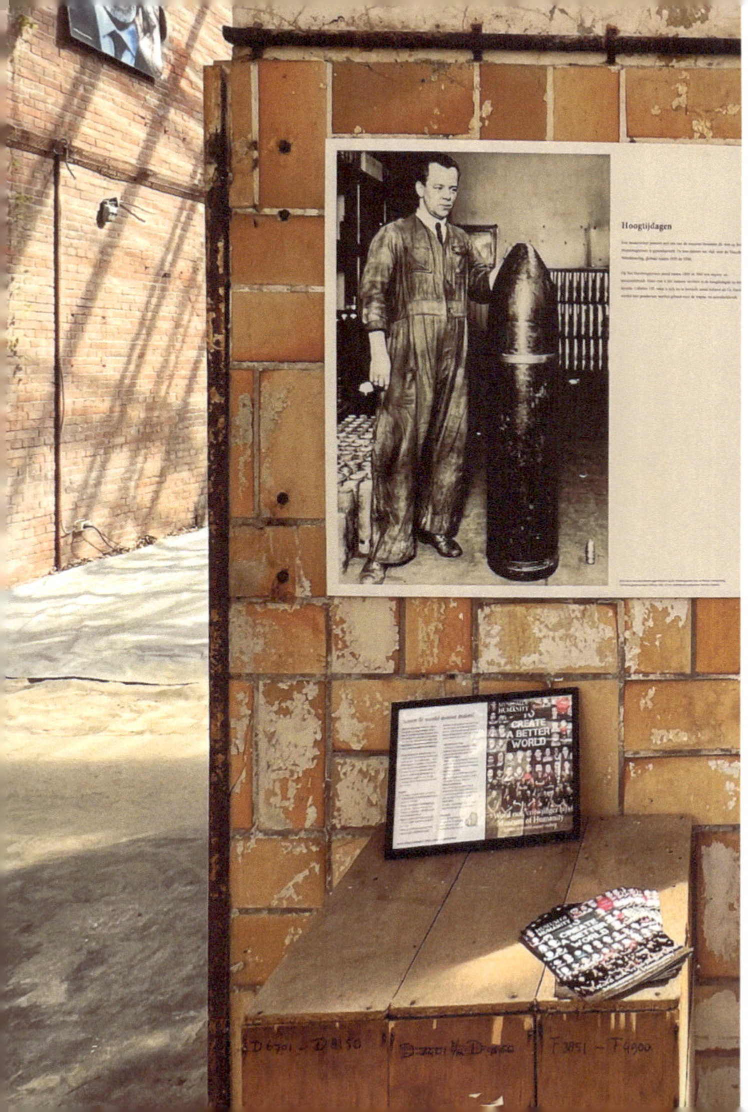
Hoogtijdagen
CREATE A BETTER WORLD
Museum of Humanity

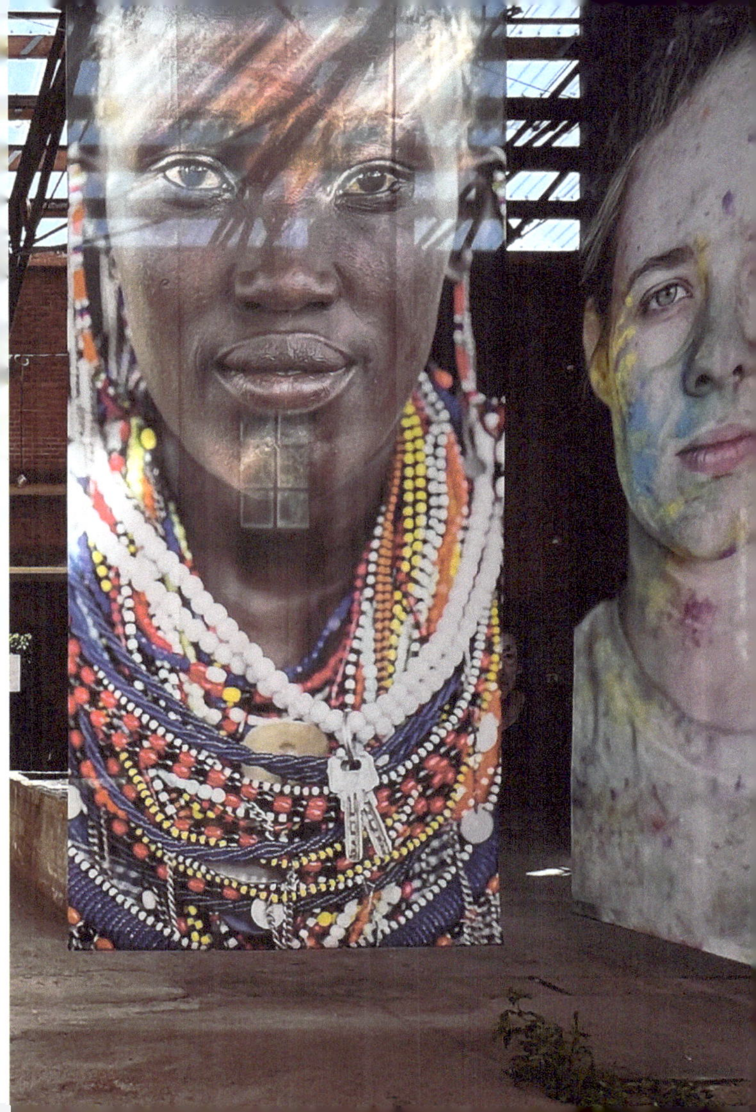

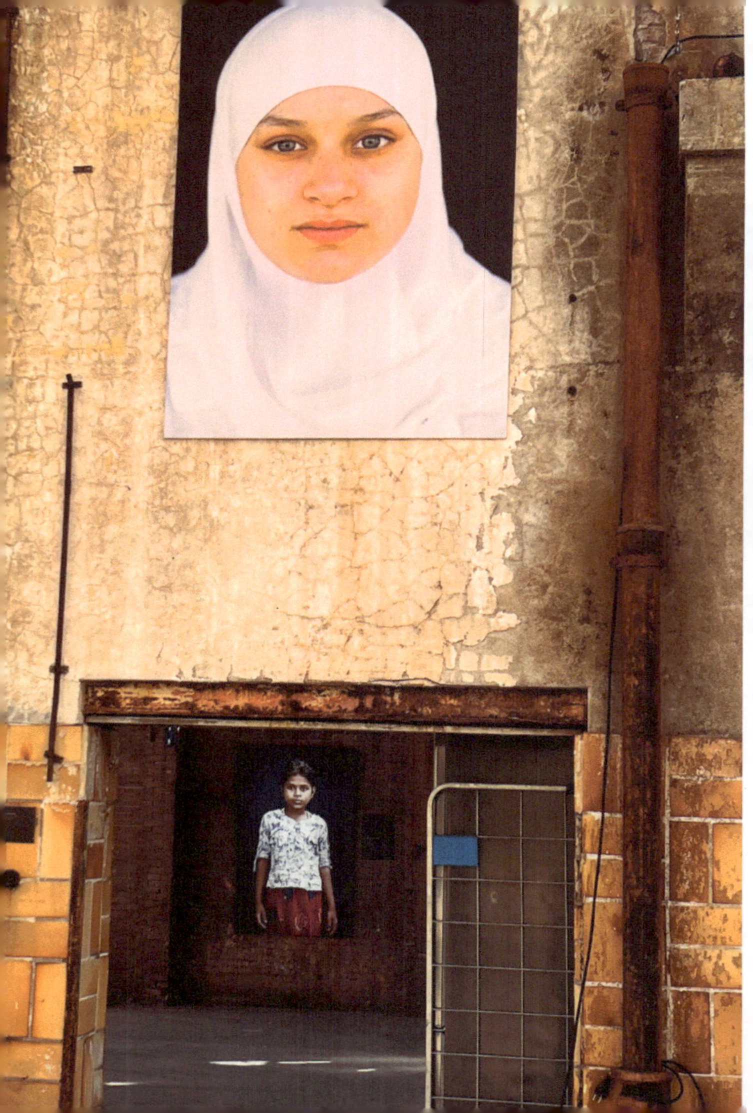

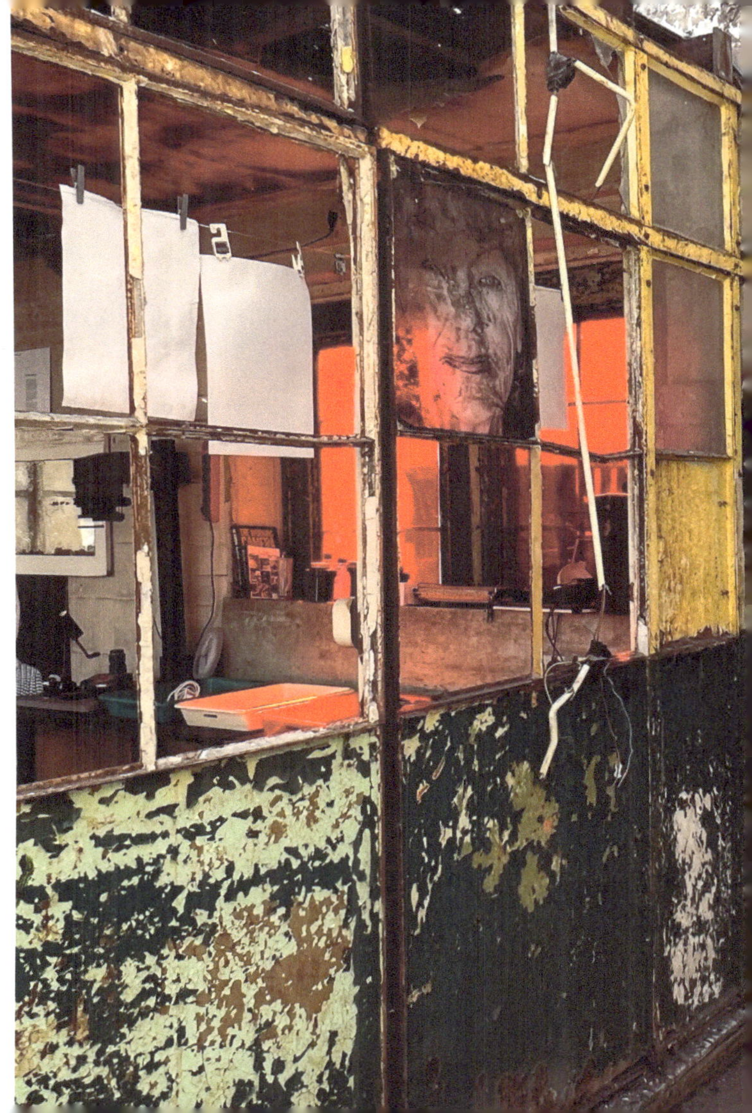

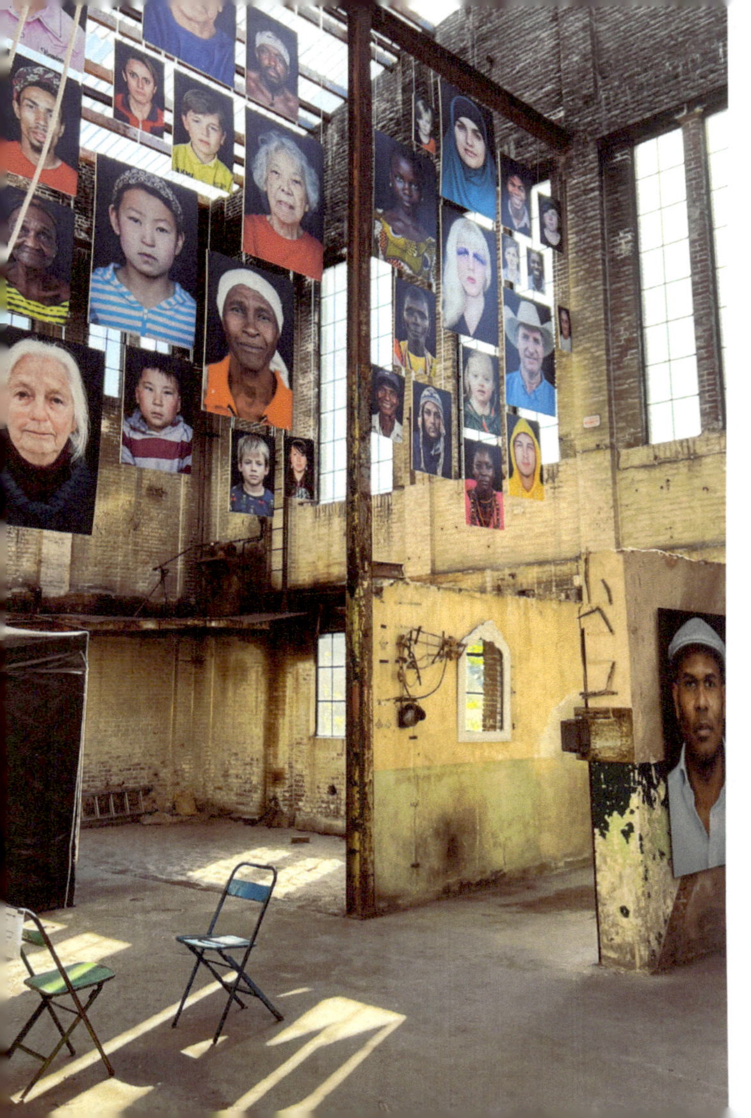

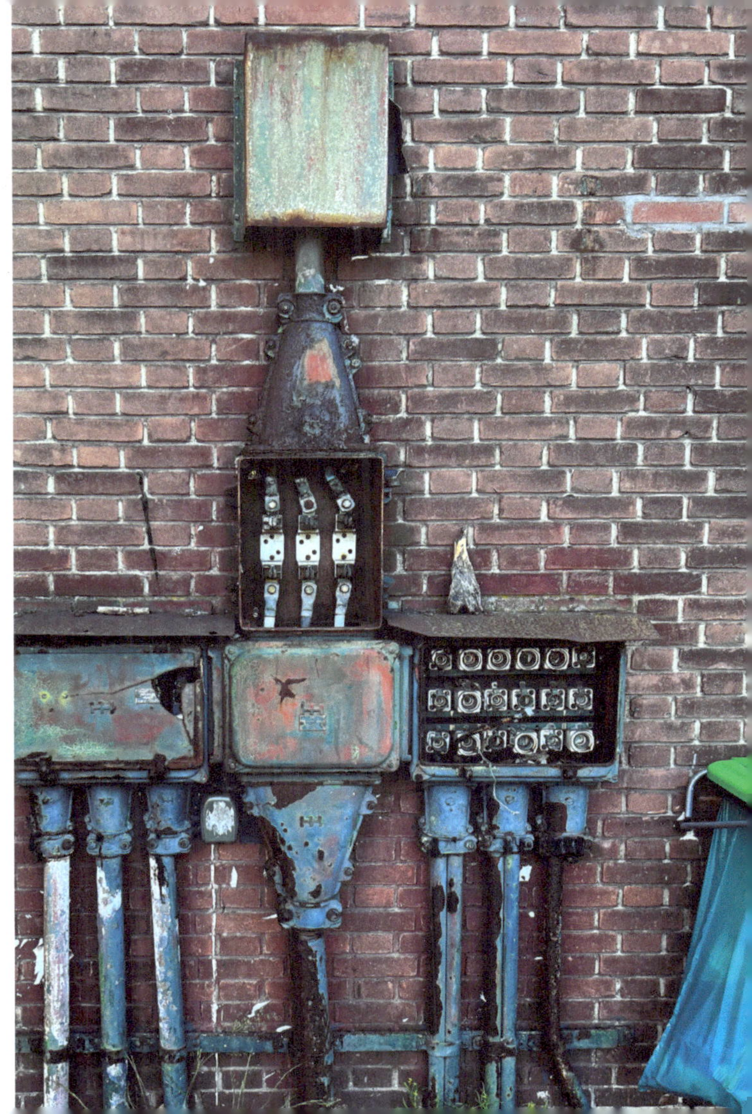

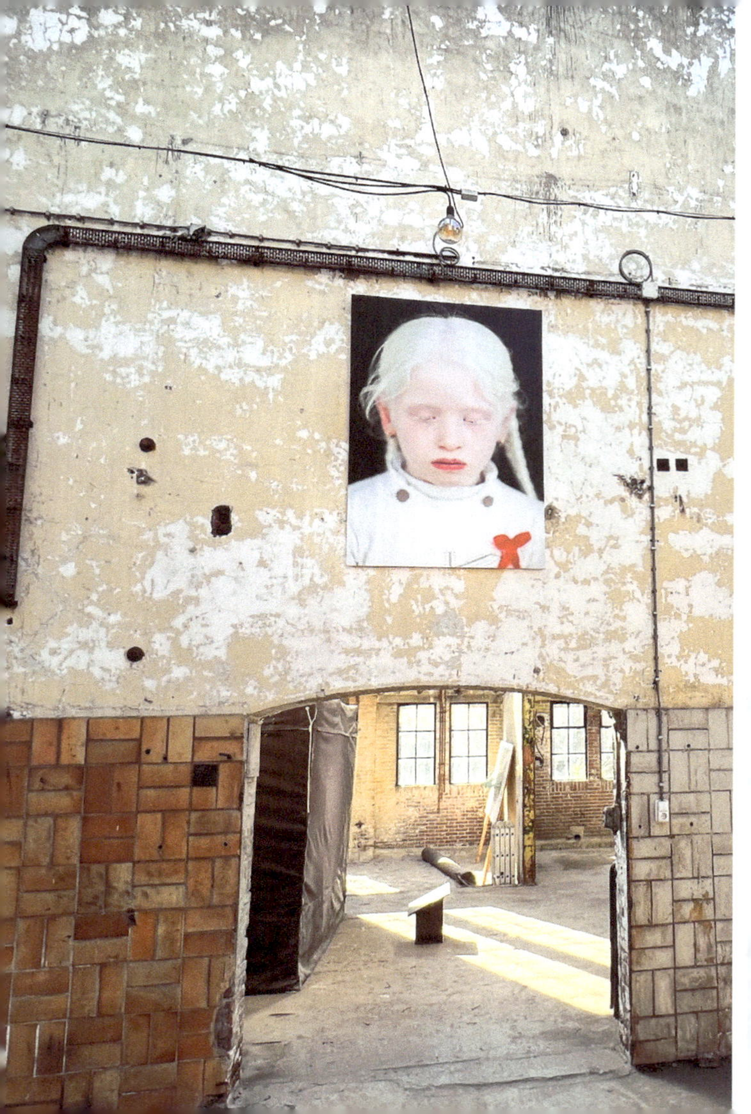

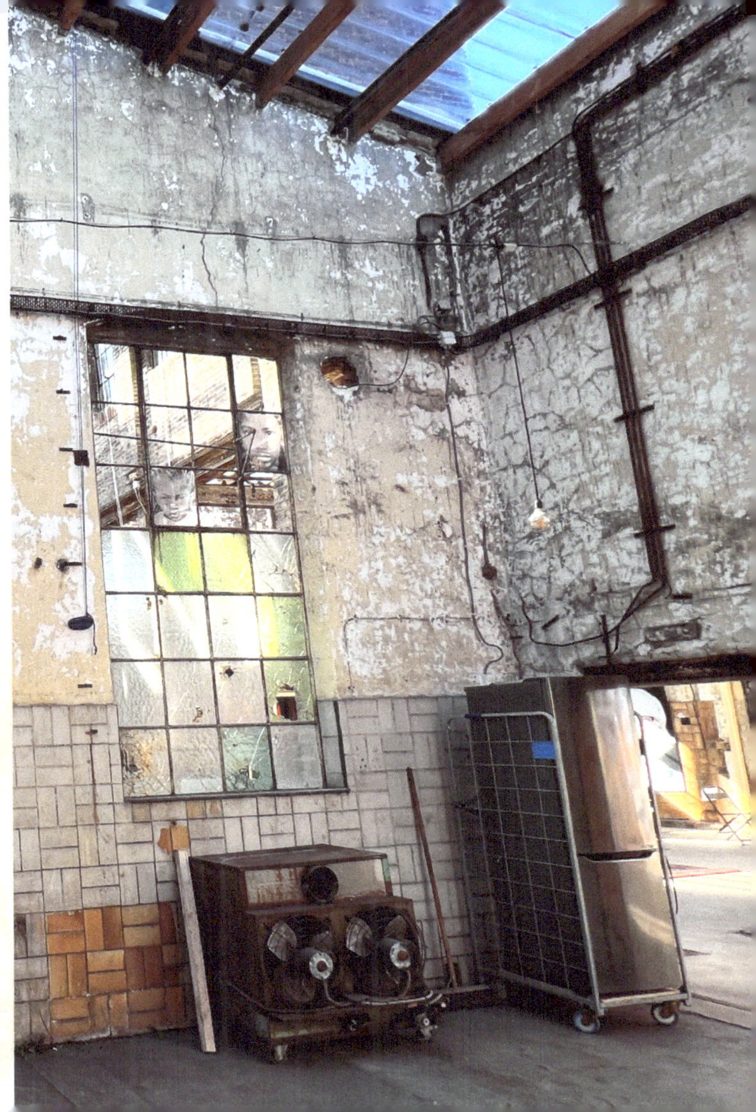

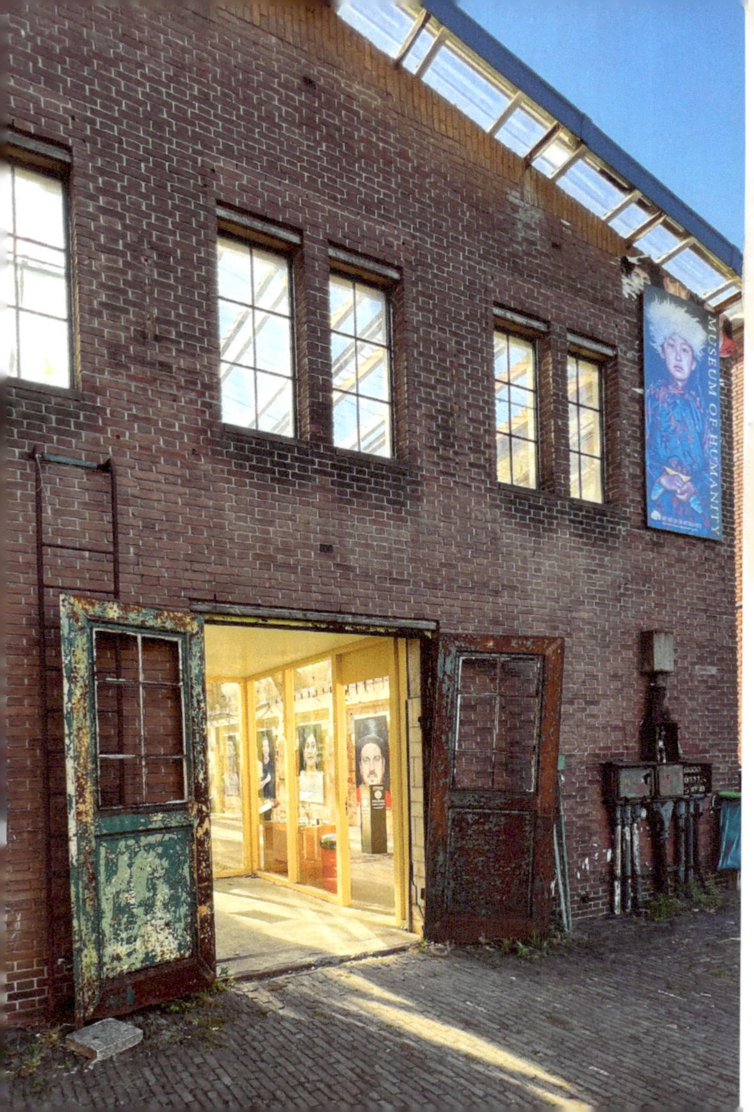
MUSEUM OF HUMANITY

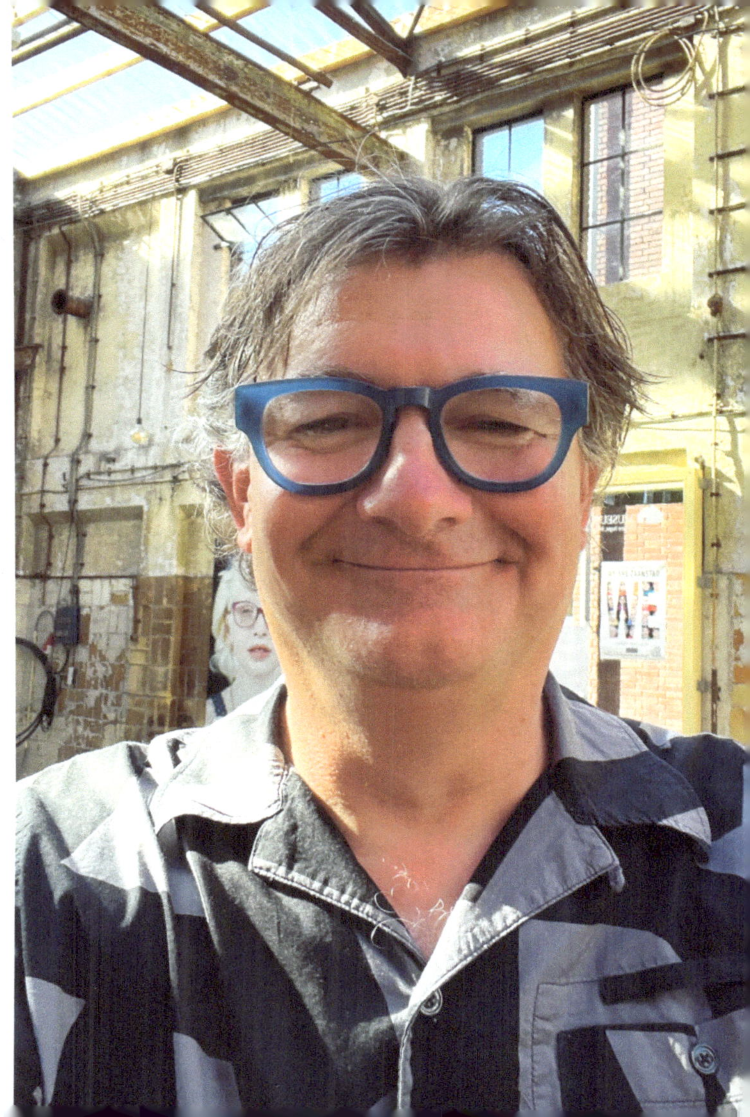

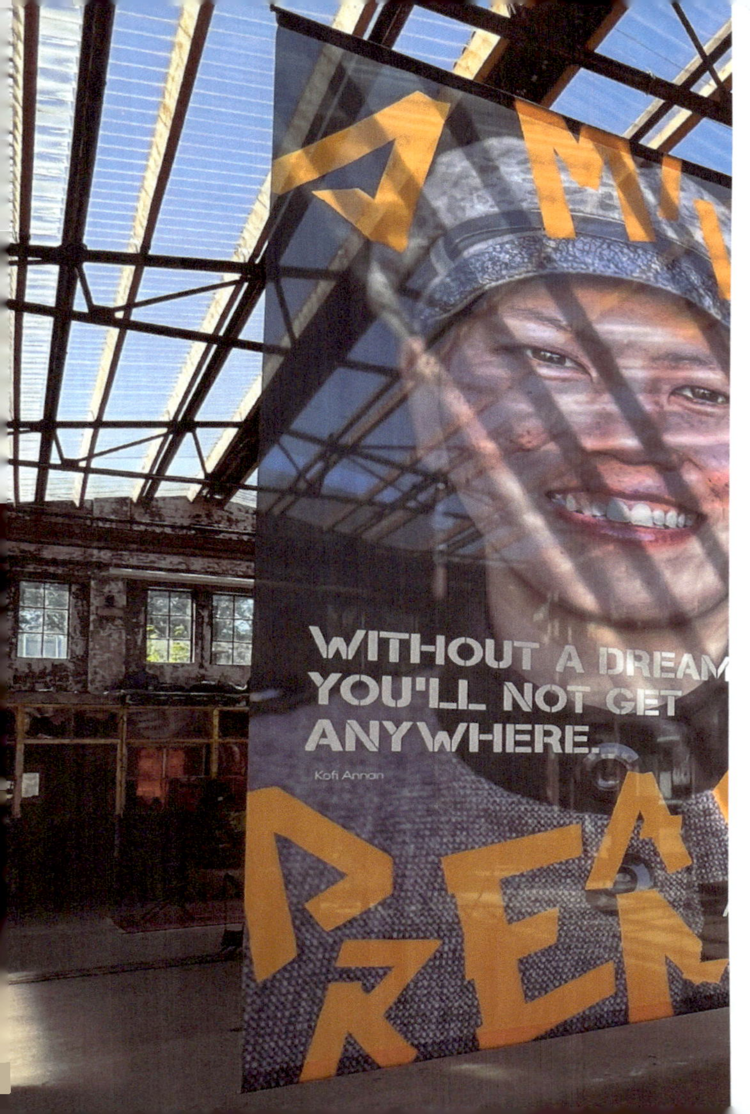
WITHOUT A DREAM
YOU'LL NOT GET
ANYWHERE.
Kofi Annan

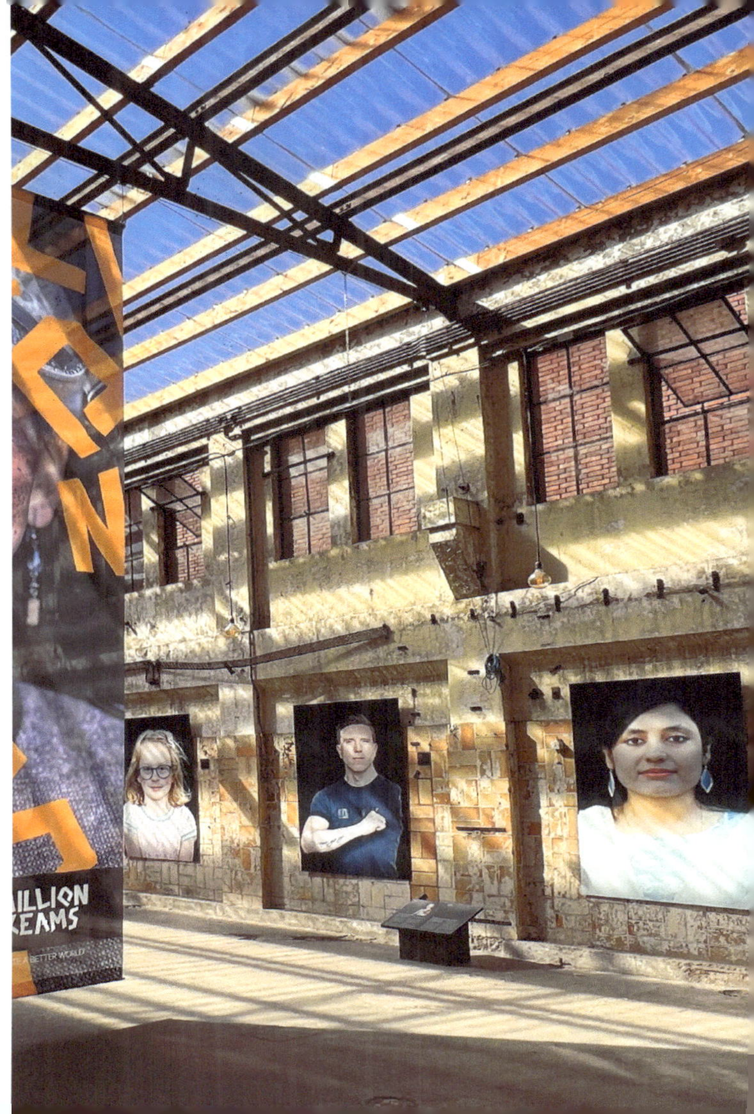
ILLION
REAMS
A BETTER WORLD

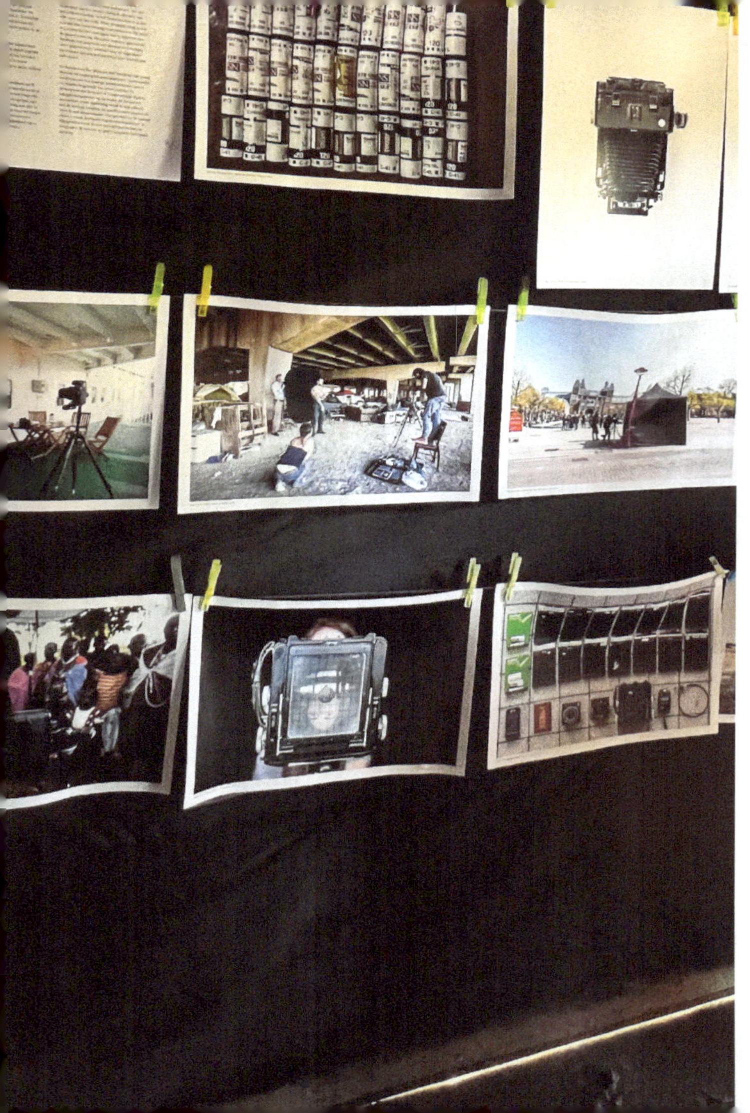

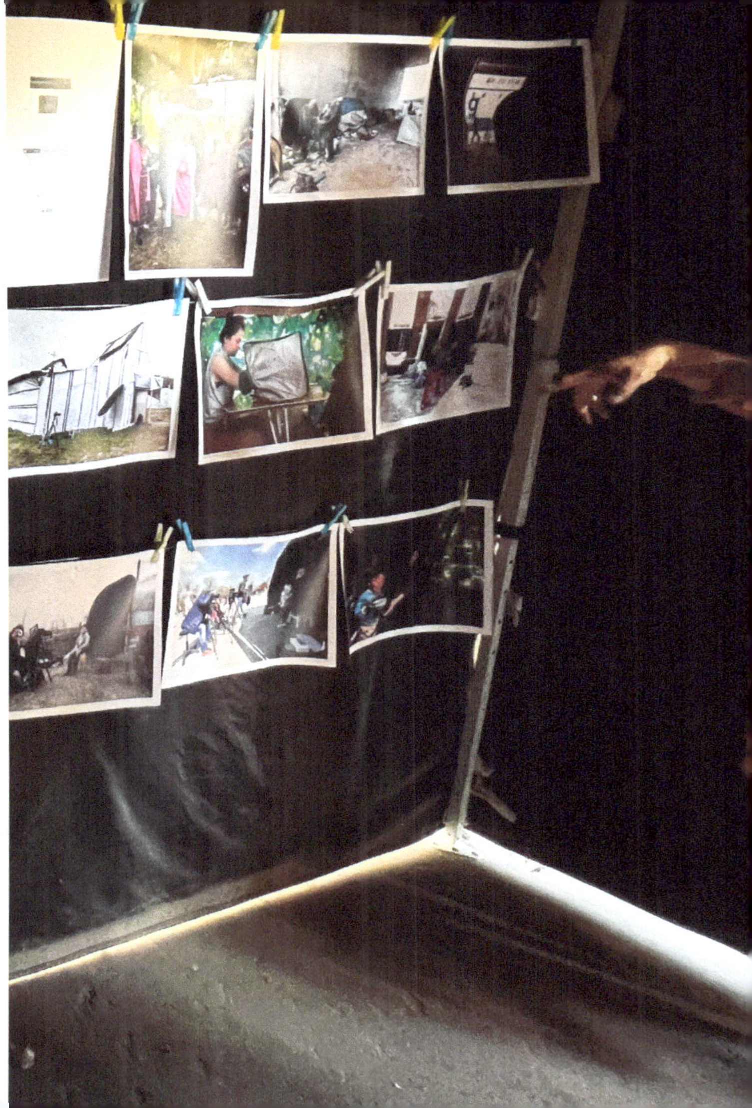

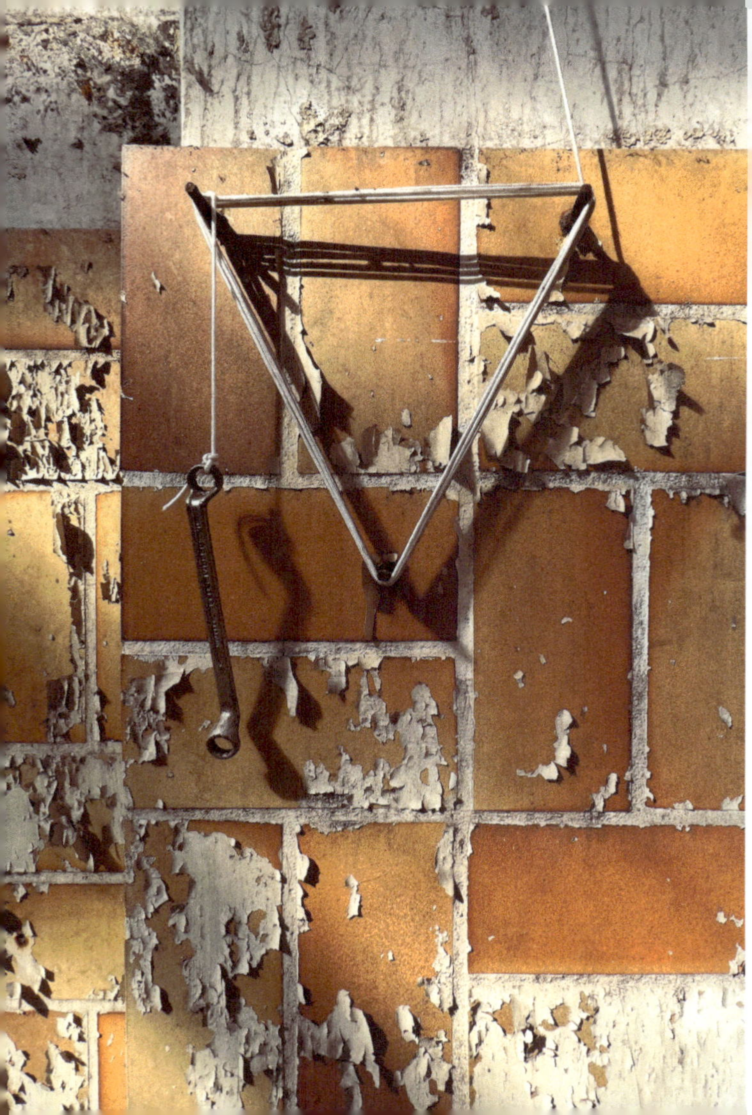

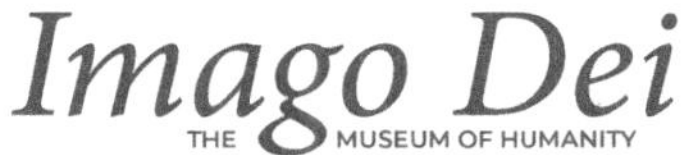

ISBN: 978-1-7371828-3-2

Photography
Tim Gilman

Book Design
timmyroland.com

Museum of Humanity
museumofhumanity.nl

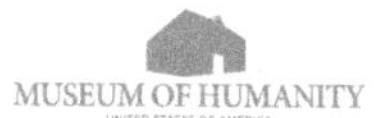